CRIME AND RECONCILIATION

CRIME AND RECONCILIATION

CREATIVE OPTIONS FOR VICTIMS AND OFFENDERS

MARK UMBREIT

Abingdon Press / Nashville

CRIME AND RECONCILIATION

Copyright © 1985 Abingdon Press

Scripture quotations noted TEV are from the *Good News Bible*, the Bible in Today's English Version. Copyright © American Bible Society, 1976. Used by permission.

Scripture quotations noted RSV are from the Revised Standard Version of the Bible, copyrighted 1946, 1952, © 1971, 1973 by the Division of Christian Education of the National Council of the Churches of Christ in the U.S.A., and are used by permission.

Scripture quotations noted KJV are from the King James Version of the Bible.

Library of Congress Cataloging in Publication Data

Umbreit, Mark, 1949-
    Crime and reconciliation.
    Bibliography: p.
    1. Criminal justice, Administration of—United States.
    2. Punishment—United States. 3. Community-based corrections—United States. 4. Reconciliation—Religious aspects. I. Title.
    HV9950.U43   1985   364.6   84-20348

ISBN 0-687-09885-8

MANUFACTURED BY THE PARTHENON PRESS AT NASHVILLE, TENNESSEE, UNITED STATES OF AMERICA

Dedicated to Alexa,
Jenny, and Laura,
the most special people in
my life.

CONTENTS

FOREWORD

For several years a syndicated news agency distributed a column I wrote called "Crime and Punishment." About twice each year I would write about capital punishment and the heavy toll it takes by fostering a sense of hatred and violence in our whole society. Articles about the death penalty brought the greatest response, with the majority of negative responses from people who identified themselves as Christians. Many of these responses contained quotes from the Bible as justification, indeed as the expectation, for *killing*, in the spirit of "an eye for an eye," those prisoners who had killed. The written cries for revenge and retribution from those readers professed knowledge neither of the availability of God's grace and forgiveness to all who sin nor of the systems of justice based on a philosophy of reconciliation and restoration which is reconciliation of the offender to his victim and his community and restoration of both, if at all possible.

The concept of justice has deteriorated in our nation today since the mid-1960s. Then the death penalty had fallen into almost total disuse, and prohibitions against the use of probation had been removed from most criminal codes. While prison populations were rising slowly (they have always risen except in time of war), the calls for community-based corrections in place of much imprisonment generally were accepted as heralding the future trend for criminal justice.

The inability of prisons and jails to punish without destroying individual self-esteem and initiative had been recognized in the early nineteenth century. Community corrections received emphasis in the recommendations of the Wickersham Commission, appointed by President Franklin Delano Roosevelt in 1933 to study crime and criminal justice. In 1935, the U.S. Bureau of Prisons director, Sanford Bates, acknowledged with regret in his book, *Prisons and Beyond,* that the rate of imprisonment in the United States far exceeded that of Western European nations. He felt that consideration should be given to a greater use of probation and other nonprison sentences, such as monetary restitution to victims and unpaid work for communities.

Most of the commission recommendations were forgotten until President Johnson appointed the Commission on Law Enforcement and the Administration of Criminal Justice in 1965. Here again the need for a greater use of community corrections was stressed as alternatives to incarceration. In 1971, still another commission was appointed, the National Advisory Commission on Criminal Justice Standards and Goals. It recommended in 1973 that in order to maximize the development of community correction programs, the nation should declare a ten-year moratorium on the construction of additional prisons. That goal never was implemented. Two years later, even though our nation still exceeded all others except South Africa and Soviet Russia in the use of incarceration—our federal, state, and local governments began the greatest building boom for jails and prisons in history.

While the Commission on Criminal Justice Standards and Goals had recommended the need for greater emphasis on social justice, rather than criminal justice, measures to reduce stranger-to-stranger crime and the political rhetoric of the decade promised otherwise: the criminal justice system, if severe enough with arrested criminals, surely would reduce crime. Thus an uninformed public led by political rhetoric and the news media, which exploited the fear rather than the facts about crime, has supported an increase in imprisonment 60 percent greater than the increase in crime in the past decade. Not only more incarceration but longer sentences and demands for the death penalty have become the norm rather than the exception.

With jail and prison construction able to provide but four new cells for every ten prisoners received, correction systems are hopelessly overcrowded. The monies needed for the social justice programs required to reduce stranger-to-stranger crime are being allocated to the wrong end of the justice system—to jails and prisons. Clearly, there is greater need than ever for leadership on behalf of a system of justice based on restoration rather than retribution. Prisoner and Community Together, Inc. is an organization providing such leadership through creative alternatives to incarceration. PACT programs joined by large and informed religious and civic leadership groups within each community will be essential if we are to have justice as fair and as considerate of the poor as it is of the affluent in our society.

Through this book, Mark Umbreit shares the experience of the organization he co-founded in 1971. Drawing upon his own religious heritage, he also addresses the broader issues of crime, victimization, and justice from a Christian perspective. Both Umbreit's leadership in PACT and his authorship of this book should contribute greatly to the ongoing national debate in both the religious and nonreligious community about how our society should respond to both offenders and victims of crime.

Milton G. Rector, *President Emeritus*
National Council on Crime and Delinquency

PREFACE

The issue of crime and punishment can trigger some of the strongest of human emotions. People who are otherwise rather peaceful and nonviolent can be brought to embrace policies of violence, repression, and even blood revenge in response to the victimization of their loved ones. Because of the powerful emotional context in which the issue of crime and victimization is rooted, responding to its presence in our communities frequently takes on simplistic forms. The issue can be boiled down easily by some to a clear definition of good guys versus bad guys. Those concerned about victims feel they must demand harsher punishments and even capital punishment for those who kill. For many, this stance is the only responsible role of citizens, and Christians specifically, in strengthening law and order within our society.

For others, the fact that the many hundreds of thousands of men and women who fill our nation's prison system are primarily the poor and the minorities causes them to reflect upon both the broader social ills that contribute to crime, and the need to respond to

13

these offenders with human compassion. For these individuals, the appropriate response for Christians and other citizens is to limit the use of incarceration, develop other forms of accountability and restitution, and work at rehabilitating and changing the behavior of these offenders.

While the former group of more traditional law-and-order advocates can easily exaggerate the presence of crime within our society and the risk that each of us faces, the latter group of more traditional offender-oriented advocates can dismiss too easily the harsh reality of crime within our society and the hurt that it causes among so many innocent victims.

If this book reinforces either one of these positions, it has failed in its most basic mission. On the other hand, if this book begins to develop a bridge between victim-oriented advocates and offender-oriented advocates, so that together they can strive for strengthening the presence of justice in our communities and the powerful message of reconciliation in such a violent and repressive criminal justice system, this book has achieved its purpose.

While the initial four chapters provide a broader perspective on the critical issue of crime and victimization, as well as our society's policy toward punishing offenders, the latter four chapters offer tangible examples of Christian leadership in responding to the needs of victims and offenders in numerous Midwestern communities. This book represents a modest attempt to bring a broader religious perspective to bear on developing a more just, humane, and healing criminal justice system. Through more than a decade of community involvement in programs with victims and offenders and the PACT organization, along with the extensive, invaluable contributions of numerous other staff and volunteers, I offer the following chapters in order to broaden our collective perspective on this difficult issue of crime and to explore the religious implications of applying the biblical principles of reconciliation and restitution.

While thanks need to be offered to many individuals who influenced me during my career and contributed to the formation of the concepts expressed in this book, the contributions of two specific colleagues must be noted. The experiences, theology, writings, and friendship of Dr. Robert B. Coates, formerly of the University of Chicago and currently the Research Director at the PACT Institute of Justice, have influenced me greatly throughout the years. Similarly, the experiences and writings of Dr. Howard Zehr, as the initial Director of the Victim Offender Reconciliation Program in Elkhart, Indiana, and currently the National Director of the Mennonite Central Committee Office of Criminal Justice, have been influential—both in sharing program development strategies and in addressing the broader issues of crime, justice, and Christian discipleship.

In addition, the assistance provided by Randy Brown, Randy Yohn, Bill Bradshaw, Donna Harling, Lyle Franzen, John Gehm, Bob Coates, and Howard Zehr in reviewing various chapters and offering helpful suggestions is greatly appreciated. I want especially to thank Donna Oglesby for her patience and endurance in typing the many manuscript pages. Most important, without the tremendous support of my wife, Alexa, and my two very precious daughters, Jennifer and Laura, I simply would have been unable to complete this project.

CRIME AND RECONCILIATION

CRIME AND PUNISHMENT
IN PERSPECTIVE

CHAPTER ONE

JUSTICE VERSUS LAW:

The Fred Palmer Story

So if you are about to offer your gift to God at the altar and there you remember that your brother has something against you, leave your gift there in front of the altar, go at once and make peace with your brother, and then come back and offer your gift to God.

(Matt. 5:23-24, TEV)

Randy and Tanya Brown returned from their honeymoon on the evening of September 23, 1976, to find that their house had been broken into. All of the wedding gifts had been stolen, and the house had been ransacked. This was the second time their home had been broken into, and Randy and Tanya experienced frustration and anger. *Why our house? How did they get in? How could anyone steal wedding gifts?* Both Randy and Tanya felt the sanctity of their home had been violated by this traumatic and unfair intrusion upon their lives.

Returning from a visit to friends on the evening of December 30, 1976, Randy and Elizabeth Yohn found that their house had been burglarized. A police officer, Randy told his family to wait in the car, grabbed his 357 Magnum handgun, and rushed into his house to find the thief. Realizing that the criminal had already left, he then surveyed his house to determine what items had been taken. The list included a TV, radios, recorders, a revolver with ammunition, and meat. As the Yohns experienced the trauma and frustration of this violation of their home, more and more questions came to their minds. *Who could have done such a thing? Why did they pick our house out of the entire neighborhood? Were they stalking us, or was our house selected randomly? Will they come back? What would have happened if we had come home while the crime was being committed? Did the criminal have a gun?*

The Browns and the Yohns were among many victims of a string of burglaries that occurred around Elkhart County in northern Indiana and an adjoining county in southern Michigan between November of 1976 and September of 1977.

The offender was eventually caught and brought to trial. Fred Palmer had not always been a criminal. As a child he had always wanted to be a priest. After attending both a Catholic school and a public school, he dropped out of high school. At the age of seventeen he enlisted in the Army and later fought in the Vietnam War. Palmer was honorably discharged in 1970, having received several commendations, including the Bronze Star.

Palmer first confronted theft because of his Vietnam unit's need to steal various equipment and supplies.

It was also during Vietnam that Palmer learned what killing other human beings is all about.

Post-Vietnam Syndrome with all of its related trauma is not simply an abstract psychological term for Fred Palmer. It became his reality upon returning to the United States in 1970. Many deep psychological scars were left upon this young soldier. His readjustment to American society was not easy.

In April of 1976, Palmer married. Despite the number of different jobs Palmer worked on, bills continued to mount and there never seemed to be enough money to make ends meet. Palmer says that he turned to burglary because he wanted his wife and daughter to have things like other people do.

In February 1978, Judge William Bontrager sentenced Palmer to ten to twenty years in prison for first-degree burglary. During the time of Palmer's offenses, Indiana was changing over to a new penal code. As Superior Court Judge of Elkhart County, Bontrager applied the spirit of the new law, which allowed him to suspend the prison sentence. He did this even though the crime had been committed during the time of the old penal code, which did not allow suspension of a prison sentence for burglary.

Judge Bontrager gave Palmer credit for one hundred fifty-nine days that he had already served in jail. In addition, the remainder of his lengthy prison sentence was suspended, contingent upon Palmer spending two hundred and five days in a maximum security prison, making restitution to his victims, engaging in psychotherapy, and remaining on probation for five years. Bontrager, known locally for his stiff sentencing, believed that a person like Fred Palmer who spends more than a year in prison is often destroyed. His

intention, as told to *Newsweek* (May 25, 1981), was to
give Palmer "a solid dose of maximum security and
then bring him back while there was still time to work
with him."

On February 23, 1978, Fred Palmer entered the
Indiana prison system. He had to adapt to the endless
boredom, loneliness, and, at times, the violence of
being caged in a maximum security prison. During this
period, Palmer experienced a Christian conversion. He
is quick to point out that his conversion was not simply
to a self-serving type of "jailhouse religion." He served
his two hundred and five days in prison with virtually
no infractions.

Following his prison release, Palmer worked regularly, although he was subject to several layoffs and
low pay for the work he was involved in. In September
1978, Palmer's probation officer referred him to the
Victim Offender Reconciliation Program in Elkhart,
Indiana, directed by Howard Zehr. Lonnie Buerge of
the Elkhart County Probation Department began to
arrange meetings between Palmer and several of his
victims. VORP allows victims the rare experience of
meeting the offender face-to-face, expressing their
feelings of frustration, receiving answers to numerous
questions, and working toward an actual restitution
agreement. Through this program, Palmer would be
able to make restitution to a number of his victims
through cash payments and actual work.

Following a good deal of initial skepticism on the part
of the Yohns, Palmer was brought together with Randy
and Elizabeth. In a rather uncomfortable and emotionally charged setting, Zehr and Buerge mediated a
discussion between these individuals, which eventually led to an agreement that Palmer would provide

cash restitution in installments to the Yohns. As a result of meeting Palmer and learning of the circumstances that led up to the crime, Randy and Elizabeth Yohn became concerned about Palmer's future welfare. In fact, during Palmer's subsequent visits in which he brought the money to Randy and Elizabeth, they got to know him better. When Randy heard that Fred had no money for Christmas gifts for his wife and daughter, he arranged the provision of numerous gifts for Fred's family so that their Christmas would be enjoyable.

The Yohns' initial bitterness and anger from being victimized slowly developed into a sense of understanding and reconciliation with the very person who had violated them. Randy would even kid with Palmer about how perhaps he should watch their home while the Yohns were on vacation.

Arranging a meeting between Palmer and the Browns was more difficult. With the bitterness of losing all their wedding gifts still fresh in his mind, Randy Brown was not too excited about being "reconciled" with Palmer. He had previously wrestled an armed robber to the ground and was interested in bringing a shotgun to any meeting with this current criminal.

"At first, I wished that I had been home so that I could have shot him," he commented during the filming of an ABC television documentary. "It's just as simple as that."

After further discussion with representatives of VORP, Randy and Tanya Brown eventually agreed to meet with Palmer.

When Palmer arrived at their home in the presence of the mediator, the Browns remained skeptical. During the meeting, they asked him a wide range of questions and openly expressed their feelings of anger and frustration. In the process, they learned that Fred Palmer was not simply a "criminal" but was a person in his own right, a father and family man. They eventually agreed upon restitution involving several Saturdays of chopping wood at the Browns' home. "When he [Palmer] left during the evening," Randy said later, "he offered his hand in friendship and I took it . . . we shook hands."

The VORP program arranged additional meetings between Palmer and several of the other families he had victimized. It was not easy for Palmer to meet eyeball-to-eyeball the very people he had violated. "When I faced my victims, it scared the living daylights out of me and it hurt. I done wrong. I would at least like to pay them back some way." His probation officer stated that "it is apparent that Fred has made extremely good efforts toward becoming a productive member of his community."

Judge Bontrager's unusual sentence in the Fred Palmer case was never accepted by the local Elkhart County Prosecutor's Office. They contested this sentence to the Indiana Supreme Court, claiming that the penal code in force at the time the offenses by Palmer were committed did not allow for suspending a prison sentence. Max Walker, from the local prosecutor's office, stated in *Newsweek*, "It wasn't like Palmer was a boy scout; he committed a dozen serious crimes." Walker and his colleagues were determined to see that the full force of the law be brought upon Fred Palmer through long-term prison incarceration.

The Indiana Supreme Court ruled, on March 23, 1979, that the trial court had no authority to suspend

Palmer's prison sentence. In August of 1979 Judge Bontrager disqualified himself from the case, publicly stating his desire to resign. Drawing upon his Christian heritage and understanding of discipleship, Bontrager is quoted in *The Christian Century* as stating there were "irreconcilable differences between the laws of Indiana and the laws of God." Despite Bontrager's intense feelings about this case and its inherent conflict with his sense of Christian discipleship, his colleagues persuaded him to stay on the bench and work within the system for further change.

As special judge, Richard H. Sproull heard the case again in September of 1979, and found that "it would indeed be a hardship upon him [Palmer] at this time to be recommitted to prison for error not committed by himself, but by the original sentencing judge [in suspending the sentence]. . . . I believe, it is, in fact, cruel to return the defendant to prison to serve an additional period of time, as he has served the term fixed by the court and has fulfilled his original sentence." However, Judge Sproull was unwilling to break new ground in this case, and he left the final decision to a higher court for review. On September 7, 1979, Judge Sproull sentenced Palmer to ten to twenty years in prison for first-degree burglary, with credit for time served. Palmer remained free in the community on an appeal bond.

In response to Palmer's appeal of Judge Sproull's ruling, Max Walker and the Elkhart County Prosecutor's Office continued to pursue the case before the Indiana Supreme Court, particularly since Palmer remained free in the community. In January of 1981, the Indiana State Supreme Court ordered Palmer to prison. On February 17, 1981, Sproull resentenced

Palmer to ten to twenty years in the Indiana prison system.

Shortly afterwards, the State Supreme Court found Judge Bontrager in indirect criminal contempt for allowing Palmer out on an appeal bond and removing himself from the case. Bontrager was.fined $500 and received a suspended thirty-day prison sentence.

One year later, Judge Bontrager resigned on an issue separate from the Palmer case. He immediately set up a Christian mediation service within the Elkhart County community and later went on to work with the Christian Legal Society in Minnesota, as well as doing consultant work for the Prison Fellowship Ministry of Charles Colson.

Palmer was again in prison, not for the commission of a new crime, nor for violation of the conditions of probation. Despite having already served more than a year behind bars and having been reconciled with his victims, Palmer had to leave his wife and two children, to return to the cold steel bars of the Indiana prison system.

Palmer himself had now become victimized by a criminal justice system that was intent on adhering to the precise letter of the law, while violating the spirit of that same law. He was being penalized for the courageous actions of a judge who placed his commitment to his religious faith above the precise technicalities of the state.

Back in prison, Palmer began working as a clerk in the kitchen. He was responsible for all of the paperwork, including the account books and payroll. In addition, Palmer conducted a Bible study group with other prisoners using correspondence courses that were made available through the Salvation Army.

Later, he clerked for the prison chaplain and got involved with the Prison Fellowship ministry, headed by Colson, which brought outside volunteers to worship and study with inmates.

Palmer's religious faith and ultimate hope for release to his family tempered his understandable bitterness at the type of justice he had received. In fact, Palmer stated that if it had not been for his strong belief in Jesus Christ and his ministry of reconciliation, he would not have been able to endure the intense feelings of frustration, anger, and alienation that he was periodically confronted with.

Palmer's family and friends, as well as his church, did not sit back quietly during this period of his reincarceration. Almost immediately, the Southside Fellowship (Mennonite and Brethren) in Elkhart and the local VORP program, through Howard Zehr, began to work on behalf of advocating clemency for Palmer to Governor Robert D. Orr of Indiana. Letters of support arrived. Numerous meetings organized additional support.

Eventually, a meeting was scheduled at the State Capitol with Judge John Ryan, the special counsel to Governor Orr on matters of clemency and a small delegation from the Southside Fellowship. Palmer's supporters from his church initially felt this meeting went fairly well. And yet, the request for clemency was denied within thirty days. It was clear that Governor Orr would make no exceptions to his normal procedure of granting clemency. Palmer would simply have to wait another year for his regular eligibility date—July 1982.

As Palmer's wife, friends at the Southside Fellowship, and numerous others waited for Fred's case to be heard before the clemency board in July of 1982, additional support mobilized. The Palmer case received widespread media attention. Several television stations highlighted the case; *Newsweek* magazine ran a feature article; and several nationwide religious journals carried articles about the case. Letters began pouring in from all parts of the country in support of Fred Palmer's clemency request.

Finally, in July 1982, the clemency hearing date was scheduled. A delegation of family, friends, members of Southside Fellowship, a victim, and a representative of the PACT organization that operates the VORP program were present at the hearing to testify. The hearing began with the chairperson showing the multitude of letters in support of Fred Palmer.

Palmer's wife stated her need for her husband to return home to her and their children. Members of Southside Fellowship testified to their experiences with Palmer as a growing Christian seeking forgiveness and reconciliation. They expressed faith in Palmer's ability to become a responsible citizen and spoke of the support that their religious fellowship would continue to provide upon Fred's release. A PACT representative spoke about the unusual nature of this case, the extremely good risk that Palmer represented in terms of being released to the community, and the continued support PACT would offer. Most significantly, Randy Brown was present to explain to the clemency board how he was victimized by Fred Palmer and initially wanted to meet him with a shotgun. Brown spoke of how he got to know Palmer as a person—how he had received restitution and became reconciled with Palmer. He stated that Palmer had been punished enough, and it was now time for him to return to his family. The delegation of Palmer's supporters left the clemency hearing optimistic yet uncertain about the outcome of their efforts.

It was not until many months later, in November of 1982, that Governor Orr granted clemency to Fred Palmer on the condition that he serve his last six months as a prisoner in a community-based work-release center. Finally, after having been reconciled with a number of his victims, having endured several periods of incarceration in both Indiana and Michigan (totaling more than two and one-half years), having endured the loneliness and alienation of being caged and removed from his family, and after years of advocacy on his behalf from various supporters throughout the country, Fred Palmer was a free man. He could now rejoin his family, as well as his religious fellowship and his community.

Ironically, the job which Palmer secured during his work-release placement was at a recreational vehicle factory partly owned by Max Walker, the prosecutor who was so intent on seeing the letter of the law implemented and the firmest punishment allowable brought upon Fred Palmer.

Unfortunately, Palmer later became separated from his wife, which eventually resulted in a divorce. His own family had now become secondary victims of the crime and punishment experienced by this troubled Vietnam veteran.

Fred Palmer's case in an Elkhart, Indiana, court is clearly not typical of the many thousands of offenders who go through our nation's criminal justice system. The manner in which he became enmeshed in a legal controversy around the new mandatory sentencing law was unique. The roles that several key people played were important: the unusually determined prosecutor who continued to press for prison punishment; the equally unusually courageous judge who was determined to implement the spirit of the law, even as it violated the letter of that law. In addition, the strong church and community support mobilized behind the case of Fred Palmer was critical.

The case does, however, raise fundamental questions about justice, faith, and Christian discipleship. Despite the uniqueness of this case, these broader questions relate to virtually all of the multitude of victims and offenders caught up in the mechanisms of our criminal justice system.

Was justice really served by pressing this case and reincarcerating Fred Palmer? Or, had justice already been served by the mere fact that victims were receiving repayment, were satisfied with the action of the court, and Palmer himself was, by any definition, rehabilitated?

At a time when our nation's prison system is bulging and the cost of incarceration is skyrocketing, what is the sense of being so determined to incarcerate a nonviolent convicted criminal like Fred Palmer? With Indiana's prison system 40 percent over capacity and under two federal court orders to reduce overcrowding, and with the clear need to have space available for more violent, repetitive criminals—why Palmer?

In responding to an offender like Palmer, does it make sound economic sense to require a punishment far more costly to the taxpaying public than the actual financial loss to his victims, while at the same time restricting his ability to further repay his victims?

At what point do Christians working within the criminal justice system say no to Caesar and render unto God what is God's? Can public officials be flexible enough to respond within the spirit of its laws in affirming the basic human needs of people, rather than relentlessly and bureaucratically pursuing the precise technicalities of these laws? How can we who are Christians more systematically apply the biblical message of reconciliation, healing, and restitution to the complexities of a repressive and violent criminal justice system?

The questions are always easier to identify than our own individual responses. In the case of Fred Palmer, the individual testimonies of Fred, Howard Zehr, Lonnie Buerge, the Southside Fellowship, William Bontrager, and numerous others clearly speak for themselves. Their courage and convictions provide guidance to those of us who continue to struggle with applying our Christian heritage of love, forgiveness, redemption, reconciliation, and hope to the enormous amount of hurt and pain experienced by both victims and offenders.

QUESTIONS FOR THOUGHT

1. In your opinion, what are the unique characteristics of the Fred Palmer story?
2. What relevance, if any, does the Fred Palmer case have to other victims and offenders involved in the criminal justice system? Are any of these known to you personally?
3. Do you think Judge Bontrager was right in violating the existing sentence codes and allowing Fred Palmer to be placed in an alternative to incarceration? Why or why not? What principles are involved?

4. Is it appropriate to allow your religious faith to surpass adherence to the letter of the law, as Judge Bontrager did? Why or why not?

5. What do you think was the motivation of the prosecutor in pressing the case of Fred Palmer?

6. In your opinion, was the prosecutor justified in pursuing this case to the Supreme Court?

7. Have you ever been burglarized? If so, how would you have initially felt toward the person who violated your home?

8. Would you have been willing to meet the burglar in the presence of a trained mediator, as many of the victims in the Fred Palmer case did? What would be the advantage to such a meeting?

9. In your opinion, was the alternative sentence that Fred Palmer received too lenient?

10. Would Fred Palmer have been held more personally accountable for his difficult behavior by a lengthy prison sentence? Why or why not?

CHAPTER TWO

CRIME IN PERSPECTIVE:

Epidemic or Media Hype?

*Ye have heard that it hath been said, "Thou
shalt love thy neighbour, and hate thine enemy.
But I say unto you, Love your enemies, bless
them that curse you, do good to them that hate
you, and pray for them which despitefully use
you, and persecute you; that ye may be the
children of your Father which is in heaven.'*

(Matt. 5:43-45, KJV)

Bob Jackson had just been released from the
repressive and violent experience of fifteen years in
prison. Two young reform-minded Christian lawyers,
Dan and Linda Smith, provided legal help and also
attempted to place Bob in a local halfway house
program. Unlike Fred Palmer, Jackson was reluctant to
trust any authority or supervision after so many years
of being caged. He was determined to make it on his

own. The Smiths helped to find him a job, and Jackson began working regularly. Dan and Linda Smith stayed in close contact with Jackson offering whatever support they could.

Jackson got in the habit of frequenting the local bar every day after work. Several weeks after his release, Dan Smith received a call one evening from a local bartender. Jackson was drunk, becoming very disruptive, and the bartender requested that Dan come over and remove him before he got into further trouble. With his wife, Linda, gone to a meeting and his daughter, Tracy, sleeping, Dan asked his neighbor to watch the house till he got back.

Jackson was indeed drunk and belligerent, but Dan was able to convince him that it was time to go home. They drove to Dan's house, where they watched a football game on TV. Dan fell asleep. Hours later, Dan was abruptly awakened by Jackson holding a butcher knife.

Bob Jackson made it clear that he would kill Dan if he did not cooperate because he was determined to run away, and he tied Dan to a chair. Dan silently prayed that Jackson's actions would not awaken his young daughter and create further violence. He convinced Jackson to let him talk to Linda when she came back from her meeting.

Linda arrived home and Dan informed her that there was a problem. He told her that Bob Jackson was determined to flee from the area and that they must cooperate.

Jackson became more hostile and aggressive. He grabbed Linda and shouted to Dan that he was taking her as a hostage and needed their car. After receiving the keys, he rushed from their apartment, with a firm grip on Linda, and sped away in the car.

As they left town and headed for a nearby state, Jackson stopped several times. Linda was raped. Jackson was ready to kill her since he thought he would get the death penalty anyway if caught. He backed off only after Linda informed him that the death penalty did not apply to rape. Even in the midst of the trauma and pain of having been raped, Linda tried to figure out how she could get out of the car.

Finally, as they were leaving the highway on an exit ramp she sighted a police car. She quickly opened her door, jumped out, and ran toward the police officer. Jackson was immediately apprehended.

Throughout the evening, both Dan and Linda had maintained as much direct eye contact with Jackson as possible in such a violent encounter. Looking back upon this tragic event, both agree that had they not been able to temper Jackson's growing hostility with direct eye contact and conversation, drawing upon their prior relationship, both of them could have been killed.

Joe and Marva Williams were at the Sunday evening service of the Baptist church in their neighborhood. In times of trouble, both were drawn even closer to their faith and their fellowship at the church. Joe had worked for eight years at the local steel mills but was now unemployed. Marva had recently lost her part-time job as a waitress. She was now receiving public assistance, and with that and the small savings they had accumulated, they were just barely able to meet their own needs and those of their six-year-old son, Bob, and three-year-old daughter, Laura.

When they arrived home from church, Joe and

Marva noticed that the front door was wide open. Following a brief period of disbelief, if not shock, they realized that their home had been broken into.

Joe told Marva and the kids to go to the neighbor's house and call the police. Joe ran inside and quickly discovered that the criminals had already left.

When the police arrived, they all went into the house to determine what had been stolen. The TV was gone. All of the dresser drawers were ransacked, many of their clothes gone. Closets were empty. The stereo was gone. The FM radio was gone. And, most significantly, the five hundred dollars that Joe had accumulated from his prior job and kept in the house was gone.

The pain and trauma that Joe and Marva Williams experienced, as they tried to tell their children what had happened, is difficult to describe. It was as if they had been raped, or a part of them killed. Times had been very rough, and yet, the few possessions that they had and the little money they were able to save were now gone. *How could anyone have done this? Why did they pick our house? Will our children ever get over being frightened? Will the criminals come back? Why us?*

For Dan and Linda Smith, as well as Joe and Marva Williams, crime statistics mean very little. The painful reality of crime had abruptly and unfairly jolted the normalcy of their lives. Crime statistics cannot bring healing to the deep psychological scars left after such violation. Nor will they help Joe and Marva Williams explain to their children why anyone could do such a terrible thing. Knowledge of crime statistics won't help them put their lives back in order.

The fact remains, however, that the trauma experienced by the Smith family and the Williams family was but a small example of the many thousands of individuals who are victimized each year in the United States. On a nationwide basis, a serious crime (murder, rape, assault, robbery, burglary, larceny, or auto theft) occurs every two seconds according to the Federal Bureau of Investigation. Placing crime in perspective requires moving beyond the tragic stories of individual victims, as well as understanding the broader public fear of crime.

There are probably few other, if any, social issues that trigger such deep human feelings as crime. Unlike many other problems in our society, crime can cut into our lives at any time and violate the safety and security that we so much need living in a complex industrialized society. The fear of being victimized can change entire life-styles and place enormous restrictions upon mobility and freedom. Crime can trigger the deepest human emotions—anger, rage, revenge, even the desire to kill those who kill others.

Public fear of crime is at an all-time high according to a recent national report. In fact, even during times in which the American public has been preoccupied with difficult economic problems, crime has often ranked as the second most critical problem that Americans are concerned about. In a recent year, *Newsweek* and *Time* magazines both devoted large sections of their magazines as cover stories, on the epidemic of crime in American society. Even more recently, the ABC television network devoted an unprecedented two weeks of air-time to focus upon crime in America.

This widespread fear of crime is rather understandable when you examine the source of the public's perception of crime. Clearly, the overwhelming source of influencing the general public's attitude toward crime is through the media. Even if you have not been victimized yourself, you cannot go a day without being bombarded by the newspapers, radio, and television with stories about criminal activity, with particular emphasis on the most violent and heinous crimes described.

The media accounts of crime cannot help but trigger intense fear. This fear, understandably, cries out for quick and simple solutions. Demands for longer sentences, less rehabilitative services, and greater use of capital punishment abound in such an emotional atmosphere. Cries for harsher punishments can become an endless thirst on the part of the general public, and politicians are well aware of it as they give their constituencies tough "law and order" rhetoric.

At this point we need to ask a critical question: does the portrayal of crime by the media reflect the actual presence of crime in our society? Is the deeply felt fear of crime in American communities consistent with the actual risk of citizens being victimized? What is the likelihood of your or my being victimized as Dan and Linda Smith were, or Joe and Marva Williams? Is there an epidemic of crime in American society? Is most crime violent and directed against persons?

The answers to these questions are mixed. On the one hand, there is, in fact, a very large volume of crime in American society. At a more human level, any single act that violates the safety or property of another citizen is wrong and harmful. On a broader level, for every 100,000 American citizens, there are 5,800 serious criminal offenses. Clearly there is a high volume of crime within our nation. Many maintain that our high level of crime and, simultaneously, the largest volume of private handgun ownership in the free world are no coincidence.

On the other hand, the best research available in the field indicates that crime has remained essentially stable over the past decade. While all of us would agree that the total volume is too high, there is little evidence that it is at an epidemic level.

Frequent headlines in magazines and news articles that shout "crime wave" or "epidemic of crime sweeping the nation" are referring to FBI crime reports. These are based on crimes reported to the FBI by local police departments and were long ago discounted by criminologists as an accurate measure of the presence of crime within our communities. In addition, the dramatic rise in crime reported by the FBI during recent years has been more a function of better police reporting procedures, particularly through computerization, rather than actual new crimes being committed. In fact, during several recent years, even these FBI reports on serious crime have indicated a leveling off, and some decreases, nationwide. (The FBI index of serious crimes is murder, rape, aggravated assault, robbery, burglary, larceny-theft, and auto theft.)

Far more accurate crime statistics have been collected by the National Victimization Surveys of the U.S. Census Bureau, utilizing statistically valid research procedures. Rather than relying upon police reports to the FBI, which in some cases were subject to political manipulation, the census bureau reports were based upon a large random sample of American households, whether the crimes were reported to police or not. From the period of 1973 through 1981, the National Victimization Survey of the Census Bureau indicated that the total level of crime remained remarkably stable, with minor increases and decreases occurring during that period, but clearly no consistent rise to epidemic levels.

A related question involves the nature of the crimes committed. Understandably, the greatest fear is directly related to frequent media reports on violent and heinous crime. Many believe that most crime in our nation is directed against people and involves various levels of violence. Yet, as we move beyond public perceptions of crime and toward a more factual perspective about the actual types of crime committed in American society, some interesting information emerges.

For the past decade, over 90 percent of all serious crime reported by the FBI has been nonviolent property-related crimes such as burglary, larceny-theft, and auto theft. Less than 10 percent of these crimes have been crimes of violence against people (murder, rape, aggravated assault, and robbery). So, contrary to common public belief, most serious crime in America is not violent. If you include less serious crimes that are not included in the FBI index categories, making the total number of crimes larger, the percentage of violent crime would be even smaller.

Homicide, the crime that is most terrifying and frightening to each one of us, represents less than one-half of one percent of all serious crime reported to the FBI. Nearly 60 percent of all homicides nationwide are committed by people who knew, if not loved, each other, and who in a fit of rage and anger ended their conflicts, usually with handguns. The fact is that we are more likely to be killed by our spouse, our friend, our business associate, or neighbor than by a total stranger who viciously robs or rapes before finally murdering us. We are also more likely to be killed on the road by a drunken driver than by the unknown, unscrupulous, unloving criminal that many of us fear.

Putting crime in a broader perspective is not meant to minimize its impact on specific individuals such as the Smiths or the Williams, nor to imply that somehow it should not be taken as seriously as it is. Quite the contrary, being victimized by crime is one of life's most difficult and traumatic experiences and needs to be taken extremely seriously both in terms of holding the offender accountable and in offering support and assistance to the victim of the specific crime. However, our response as a society to crime ought not to be based on an overreaction to the relatively small portion of violent crime. It should instead be based upon a more realistic assessment of the much broader presence of property and nonviolent crime in our society while still recognizing the existence of a significant but much smaller level of violent crime.

It is particularly important to recognize that those heinous crimes, such as the well-publicized Charles Manson or John Gacy killings, represent extremely rare occurrences in American society. The problem is that because they are examples of mass murder, they receive a disproportionate amount of public attention and media exposure. Whether or not we as a nation are actually experiencing an epidemic of crime or simply continued media overdramatization of the relatively small portion of violent crime remains a critical question, although the evidence certainly tends to point to the latter.

The role that Christians can play in responding to the critical needs of individual crime victims is certainly not a question. Rather, it is a vital ministry long overdue. In fact, much that the church has learned in responding to the needs of persons experiencing grief over the deaths of loved ones can be applied particularly to victims of violent crime.

When Linda Smith was kidnapped and raped before leaping from the car of her attacker into the safety of a police car, a part of her personhood died. The security and safety of her unmolested life in her community was gone. The violations she endured struck like a dagger into the fabric of her self-confidence and self-image. The trauma of being raped left psychological scars that took years to heal.

As with those grieving the loss of loved ones, it is not unusual for victims to immediately experience a sense of denial, as if this horrible intrusion into their lives really had not occurred. During this period, victims frequently can be disoriented and appear to others as if nothing really significant occurred in their lives.

Once victims begin working on their traumatic experiences and begin reintegrating their pre-offense life-style with their post-offense reality, large mood swings occur. One day they might be optimistic and apparently successful in accepting this terrible violation of their lives. The next they might be deeply depressed and isolated from all who care about them

Just as with individuals facing terminal illness, a certain amount of bargaining occurs. "If only the criminal is sent to prison or killed, then I will feel better." Even for those victims who see their offender punished severely, they well may find that the deeper psychological scars have not been healed and the trauma continues to be relived.

There is clearly a need to place the highly emotive

and media-hyped issue of crime in a broader, more factual, perspective; yet, in doing such, there could be a real danger in overlooking the enormous pain and brokenness that is found in the wake of any single, violent criminal act. As Christians, individually and through our congregations, we must not fall into this trap.

QUESTIONS FOR THOUGHT

1. As a private citizen frequently exposed to the mass media's reporting of crime, do you feel as though crime continues to rise at an epidemic level? Give reasons for your view.
2. Are you afraid to walk in your neighborhood at night?
3. Do you feel as if you have a high probability of being personally victimized?
4. Are most crimes committed in the United States violent and against persons?
5. Do you believe that media reporting of crime is balanced and provides the public with an accurate perspective on crime?
6. Is the media attention given to particularly violent crime reflective of the actual presence of violent crime in our society?
7. Do you believe that crime is committed primarily by the poor and minorities?
8. What do you believe is a relatively accurate perspective on crime in America?
9. How many times have you been victimized by such street crimes as robbery, theft, burglary, and mugging?
10. How many times have you been victimized by such white-collar crimes as price fixing, industrial

waste and chemical dumping, pollution, and faulty and unsafe consumer products?

11. What conclusion can you draw from your answers to questions 9 and 10? What can you do about both kinds of crime?

CHAPTER THREE

PUNISHMENT IN PERSPECTIVE:

Too Lenient or Too Harsh?

> The teachers of the Law and the Pharisees
> brought in a woman who had been caught
> committing adultery. . . . They said to Jesus
> . . . "Moses commanded that such a woman
> must be stoned to death. Now, what do you
> say?" . . . He said to them, "Whichever one of
> you has committed no sin may throw the first
> stone at her." . . . He said to her, "I do not
> condemn you either. Go, but do not sin again."
>
> *(John 8:3-11, TEV)*

Bob Jackson received a thirty-year sentence for
having assaulted Dan Smith and kidnapped and raped
Linda Smith. Prior to committing this crime, Jackson
had already spent more than fifteen years behind bars.
Many would consider him to have become institution-
alized, incapable of living responsibly in a free society.

47

Years after their victimization, Dan and Linda Smith had ambivalent feelings about the punishment of Jackson. On the one hand, they were grateful for the lengthy sentence that Jackson received. No longer would he be able to terrorize them or their children. Because of their familiarity with prison life, the young activist lawyers were acutely aware of how little impact such lengthy prison incarceration would have on changing Jackson's behavior. They knew that he, along with 98 percent of all other prisoners, eventually would be released. Even the thought of this inevitable reality brought fear to them.

On the other hand, Dan Smith increasingly questioned the impact of Bob Jackson's prior lengthy incarceration on their victimization. By all indications, Jackson had never been offered any help in correcting his hostile behavior. He was not placed in any creative alternative programs. His life exhibited a continuous pattern of incarceration and reincarceration. The violence and hostility of being caged created increasing bitterness and anger in the very fabric of his personality. Was he not becoming a walking time bomb? Why would the prison release him on parole?

Dan Smith could not help asking why Jackson would have turned on the very people who were trying to help him. He had a job, friends to support him, and the real possibility of growing beyond the bitterness of his past.

Why did he do it? Wasn't the punishment of fifteen years prior incarceration in maximum security prisons enough to deter him from ever committing another crime? And then, Dan Smith thought, what if Jackson had received help at an earlier age? What if he had been given the opportunity to receive psychological counseling, vocational education, and the ability to repay the victims that he had violated? Would he still have hurt us so badly? Dan Smith had to question whether the extensive prison punishment of Jackson contributed to the violence and brutality that both he, and his wife Linda, suffered.

Following twelve burglaries, Fred Palmer was locked up for a year in prison, and then released to make restitution to several of his victims. In the process he became reconciled with many of the people he had violated, and established himself in the community and with his church fellowship. Palmer eventually was reincarcerated for another year (potentially ten to twenty years) because of Judge Bontrager's technical error. The law clearly required that Palmer receive ten to twenty years of prison incarceration. Yet, if Judge Bontrager had not courageously granted Palmer an alternative sentence, would his victims have been more satisfied? Would they have been able to meet this young decorated war veteran, family man, and Christian who had done them wrong but was still a person struggling in his own way to make it in American society? Would the numerous questions and fears that these victims experienced from having the sanctity of their homes violated and their property stolen have been answered and expressed? With Palmer behind bars for ten to twenty years, would his victims have experienced a more intense sense of justice?

From all of the evidence in this actual case, the answer certainly appears to be a resounding *no*. This is particularly evidenced by the actions of two of Palmer's victims. Major Randy Yohn, now the Support Services Commander of the Elkhart County Sheriff's Department, not only became a friend to Palmer, but also

went on to become the chairperson of the local board
that supervises VORP in Elkhart, Indiana. Randy
Brown spoke on behalf of Palmer's request for
executive clemency, which later led to Governor Orr's
favorable response.

Just as it is important to place crime in a broader
perspective, moving beyond our emotional perceptions
to a factual assessment of actual risk, it is equally
important to put punishment in a more factual
perspective. Clearly, the polls indicate that the general
public, including the Christian community, feel that we
as Americans are far too lenient. It's time to get tough!
The politicians frequently exploit this fear at election
time. Never in the past decade has there been such
widespread fear resulting in the conviction that criminals
must be punished severely. A growing number of states
have passed harsh mandatory sentences, and the
number of offenders waiting to be executed has grown.
In 1979, there were approximately four hundred men
and women on death row. Today, there are well over
1,200 individuals waiting to be executed.

Is America really too lenient with criminals? When
you look at our nation from a broader international
perspective, some rather astonishing facts emerge.
While Americans might feel they are pussycats with
criminals, the actual punishment suggests otherwise.
How many Americans would be proud of the fact that
they lock up more criminals per capita than any nation
in the free western world? Only the totalitarian and
racist regimes of the Soviet Union and South Africa
exceed the U. S. rate of incarceration.

The U. S. gives out the longest and harshest prison
sentences in the free world, with an average length of
incarceration of twenty-one months. (The average is

three months in Sweden and less than one month in the Netherlands.) And at a time when the international movement among free and democratic societies is clearly away from use of capital punishment, America appears to be standing alone in advocating massive and routine use of capital punishment.

From an international perspective, Americans are certainly not too lenient. Many Europeans have a difficult time understanding the harshness of our responses to punishing criminal offenders. And yet, we cannot simplistically suggest that direct comparisons can be made between the characteristics of smaller more homogeneous societies, particularly Sweden and the Netherlands, and the complex and pluralistic characteristics of America. There are certainly significant cultural distinctions between different nations within the free and industrialized world. Yet are those cultural differences between our friends and allies sufficiently significant to explain the fact that the U. S. incarcerates twice the number of offenders per capita as Canada, three times the number as Great Britain, and four times the number of offenders per capita as West Germany?

The frequent use of incarceration in American society clearly reflects the fact that prison is a well-established form of punishing more serious crime. It is commonly believed that prisons primarily contain the most violent and repetitive criminals in our system (i.e., the real losers). Contrary to this widespread public belief, however, approximately 50 percent of the over 500,000 men and women locked up in jails and prisons across this nation have committed nonviolent crimes. Many have been convicted of no prior offenses, nor have they ever been incarcerated before. For example, recent statistics show that 27 percent of prisoners in the overcrowded Illinois system have no prior convictions. There are literally many thousands of prisoners who have been convicted of relatively minor property-related offenses, such as common theft.

The fact that prisons are overwhelmingly filled with the poor and a vastly disproportionate number of minority offenders is well known and perhaps even rationalized by some who believe that it is primarily the poor and minorities who commit the crimes. While it is true that the poor and the minorities do, in fact, commit a disproportionate number of street-crime offenses that result in prison sentences, this does not mean they somehow have a monopoly on crime.

Quite the contrary, white-collar crime committed by the well-to-do and well-connected is eleven times more costly than street crime. It is rarely dealt with seriously and rarely results in prison confinement. In most respects, American citizens lose far more money through corporate crime such as price fixing than they would ever lose through an individual act of criminal violation. Yet because corporate crime is more removed from us (and committed by "respectable" people), it is understandable that citizens are not as frightened by such costly corporate crime.

While it is true that white-collar crime is far more costly, some would claim it certainly is not violent and does not threaten our lives the way street-crime does. However, certain types of corporate and industrial crime can hardly be considered less violent than an assault or even a rape. For example, the all too frequent offenses of chemical waste dumping by businesses who wish to maximize their profits by taking the easy way out is certainly a significant threat to the health and safety of American citizens. As toxic wastes seep into the water tables, they can affect the health of an entire community. Birth defects and even eventual death may result from toxic chemical waste entering the water table that communities depend upon for their survival.

Few people realize that far more individuals are killed each year from industrial accidents than from all homicides. Certainly, many of these industrial accidents could be prevented through better safety precautions. Why is it when a mineshaft collapses and twenty-five miners are killed after the company has ignored a long series of warnings and safety violations, this is considered an "accident?" On the other hand, a distraught and emotionally depressed husband comes home, kills his family, and is considered a mass murderer. Clearly, the man killing his family committed an ugly and inexcusable deed and is, in fact, a multiple killer. But should the company responsible for the mineshaft break be held any less criminally accountable? Perhaps we could even argue they are more responsible and in need of punishment since the act resulted from such a clear, rational pursuit of profit and often with prior knowledge of unsafe conditions for the workers. Needless to say, there are few industrial criminals or white collar criminals within our nation's prison system.

Are Americans too lenient or too harsh with criminals? Ironically, the answer is found in both responses. On the one hand, our nation's criminal justice system appears quite lenient, with a high tolerance level for certain types of both nonviolent and violent crime, if committed by certain classes of individuals. When Charlotte Hullinger, co-founder of the Parents of Murdered Children organization, learned that the young man who bludgeoned to death her nineteen-year-old daughter Lisa received a six-month prison sentence, did she encounter justice? How can anyone claim that the frequent response to an industrial crime, a white-collar crime, or even a robbery committed by a fairly well-connected upper-class individual is not too lenient? How can any of us not believe that the way drug czars and Mafia criminals beat the system through payoffs, bribery, and high-powered attorneys is not too lenient?

In fact, the two crimes that literally kill the most Americans and steal the largest sums of money from us (drunken driving and white-collar crime) are dealt with quite leniently. While the media likes to report bizarre and heinous murders, the fact remains that more Americans are killed each year as a result of drunken driving than all the criminal homicides put together. While tougher laws related to drunken driving are passing, the offense is still perceived more as an unfortunate occurrence than a serious and deadly crime, with punishments being rather lenient. As mentioned previously, white-collar offenses are eleven times more costly than street crime, yet are not dealt with very seriously.

It is clear that the American criminal justice system is tolerant and lenient with certain offenders. However, the full intensity of the vengeance and wrath that many Americans feel is certainly exercised through penalties that other criminals receive. No one disputes the fact that we use incarceration extensively for those who are "the least among us," as seen by the fact that prisons remain disproportionately filled with minorities and the poor. No one disputes the fact that there is a ground swell of support for executing more and more criminals, particularly those who kill others and also represent the "least among us." When it comes to street crime, violations that directly threaten our property and lives, our system of justice is harsh for many of those who are finally apprehended, convicted, and sentenced.

The critical question is not whether there should be some form of punishment for criminal behavior. Rather, the key question is, how can criminal violators, rich and poor, be held accountable so that those committing more serious, violent offenses receive harsher penalties, while those committing nonviolent and less destructive offenses receive more moderate penalties? Does it make sense to punish a $300 thief with $15,000 of prison punishment, while the victim receives no repayment? Does it make sense to continue to pack a large volume of nonrepetitive and nonviolent criminals into already overcrowded prison facilities, thereby necessitating early release of violent and repetitive offenders? Was not the biblical directive of "an eye for an eye" to bring proportionality into the justice system, so that the punishment given the offender does not exceed the damage caused to the victim?

QUESTIONS FOR THOUGHT

1. Are Americans too lenient in punishing criminals?
2. What does *punishment* mean?
3. What does *leniency* or *harshness* mean in terms of applying punishment?

4. How does the United States rank with other free and industrialized nations in punishing criminals with prison incarceration?
5. What benefits do victims of crime receive from prison incarceration?
6. Are there benefits that victims can receive from other forms of punishment?
7. What role should punishment play within the criminal justice system?
8. What role should rehabilitation play within the criminal justice system?
9. What is a relatively accurate perspective on American policies of punishing criminals?
10. What does being punished as a criminal mean?

CHAPTER FOUR

PRISON OVERCROWDING:

The Need for Alternatives

"You have heard that it was said, 'An eye for an eye, and a tooth for a tooth.' But now I tell you: do not take revenge on someone who wrongs you."

(*Matt. 5:38-39, TEV*)

With widespread public fear of crime and frequent cries for harsher punishment, our nation's prison system has become increasingly overcrowded. Fred Palmer and Bob Jackson were simply two of the nearly half a million people behind bars on any given day in the United States.

Prison overcrowding in the United States is out of control, with the cost of continued prison construction and maintenance skyrocketing at a time of dwindling public resources. More than thirty states are under federal court orders related to overcrowded institutions and unconstitutional conditions of confinement. From 1973 to 1981 there was a 60 percent increase in the incarceration of offenders. Few states have escaped the dilemma of prison and jail overcrowding, with its related human and economic cost. As just one example, Indiana continues to operate its prison system at 40 percent over its rated capacity and is under two different federal court orders to reduce its prison population.

Many states have adopted very unusual, if not questionable, procedures for responding to this dramatic level of overcrowding. Prisoners are being housed in tents and tin sheds in Texas. Hallways, lavatories, and storage rooms are now being used as sleeping space for prisoners in New Jersey. A number of states are cramming three or four inmates into cells designed for fewer prisoners, as well as placing bunk beds in the walkways in front of cells.

Clearly, I am not suggesting that we tear down all our prisons, nor that we build new luxurious ones that are "country clubs." And yet, it's time that individuals who frequently advocate simplistic, knee-jerk responses to crime, such as building more prisons and giving longer sentences, be held accountable for such rhetoric. Ironically, such "get tough" rhetoric is remarkably similar to many traditional liberal responses to social problems that many of these same individuals would be quite critical of. Simply throwing millions of dollars of taxpayers' money at the problem of crime, in order to increase prison construction, is little different than throwing millions of dollars at welfare bureaucracies, during the War on Poverty days. Anybody who adheres to a basically conservative philosophy of public expenditure must question seriously the wisdom of such popular "get tough" rhetoric. Who can responsibly suggest throwing away millions of dollars, despite the gut feeling of many Americans that something positive will result.

There is little evidence that prisons have anything to do with reducing crime in our society, let alone rehabilitating criminals. What they are able to do is temporarily remove criminals from our communities, and this function is necessary for some who are incarcerated. It's a common illusion, however, that prisons are filled with primarily murderers, rapists, robbers, and other repetitive violent criminals, making early release from prison or diversion into an alternative simply unacceptable. Despite this common misperception, the fact remains that about half of the over 500,000 locked up in our nation's prison system are convicted of nonviolent property offenses.

On a national scale, approximately 50 percent of those incarcerated represent nonviolent offenders. In fact, according to a recent study, the proportion of violent offenders in prison dropped from 52 percent to 47 percent between 1974 and 1978. An increasingly large percentage of admissions to prison for less serious crimes exists. For example, during a recent year, 38 percent of all prison commitments in Indiana represented the lowest level felony offenses such as common theft and bad checks. There were many more admissions representing other nonviolent offenses as well. Similarly, Illinois recently had 30 percent of their admissions from the least serious property offenses.

Is prison the only appropriate punishment for these nonviolent property offenders? Who can argue the wisdom of punishing a $200 thief with $30,000 of prison punishment (and the victim doesn't even get his or her $200 back). Doesn't it make sense to first meet the needs of victims seeing that they are repaid and then identify other ways of holding nonviolent offenders accountable for their actions so that they can go on and lead productive community lives?

The economic cliché of "there's no such thing as a free lunch" is highly relevant to any discussion of prison overcrowding and alternative punishments or penalties. To suggest that we simply build more prisons (at a cost of up to $60,000 per bed to build and up to $30,000 a year to maintain) is to adhere to an economic philosophy that was rampant in the 1960s War on Poverty era. Then, the federal pie could always be enlarged. Budgets got bigger and bigger. Taxpayers paid more and more. Clearly, those days are long gone. The pie is not getting bigger. In fact, government budgets now experience tight restrictions, if not outright cuts in certain areas.

Anyone who advocates building more prisons in response to overcrowding, as opposed to developing appropriate alternative forms of punishment, must be willing to accept that for each prison constructed for millions of dollars, there is that much less money available for other important public services, such as maintaining quality education, serving those with handicapping conditions, meeting the needs of the elderly, or even paving state roads. The point is, with the current economy, we cannot have it both ways. Every dollar put into building more prisons is a dollar taken away from meeting other vital public needs.

Should we not accept the fact that prisons are finite resources? Isn't it time that Americans become better stewards of this scarce resource by being more selective of who should receive the ultimate and costly punishment of incarceration? Is the only legitimate form of criminal punishment caging the offender? Are there not other legitimate forms of punishment as well?

In many communities, judges are faced with only the two extremes—prison on the one hand as the most punitive and probation on the other hand as too lenient. That is the whole point of developing a range of intermediate alternative sanctions or penalties ranging from work release centers and halfway houses to nonresidential programs such as community service work programs where free labor is provided to local jurisdictions and direct victim restitution programs. Many alternative penalties are far more restrictive and demanding on the offender than simply probation, which can often be perceived as a slap on the hand. Yet, they only cost a fraction of what it costs to lock someone up for years in prison. Also, the offender avoids becoming a victim him or herself of the periodic assaults and rapes that too frequently occur within our "correctional facilities."

While alternative programs exist in numerous parts of the country, two specific examples should be illustrative. The PACT organization (Prisoner and Community Together) operates a Community Service Restitution Program as an alternative to jail in several counties of Indiana. For each day of his or her jail sentence, the offender must perform six hours of unpaid community service work. In one of these counties, during a recent year, over 40,000 hours of free work was provided to sixty community agencies, including governmental and nonprofit organizations.

As a form of symbolic restitution to the community whose laws were violated, this program resulted in 8,300 days being diverted from jail incarceration, at an economic value (or benefit) to the county in excess of $300,000.

VORP (Victim Offender Reconciliation Program), operated by PACT in several different communities of the Midwest, involves a face-to-face meeting between the victim and offender in the presence of a trained mediator. During this meeting the facts and feelings of the case are discussed and a restitution agreement worked out. Nearly $22,000 of restitution was agreed upon in one of these programs during a recent year. Of all victims contacted, 68 percent were willing to meet their offender. More than 80 percent of all agreed-upon restitution has been paid through VORP. This represents an unusually high rate of payment since restitution throughout the country is frequently ordered by the court but not always collected. (Both the Community Service Restitution Program and the VORP program operated by the PACT organization are described in more detail in chapter 6.)

Developing effective community-based programs to serve as viable alternative penalties for selected offenders in communities throughout the nation is critical. For without the existence of such alternative programs, judges remain faced with the extremes of either prison or probation. And yet, of equal importance is the growing recognition that such alternative programs must serve as real substitutes for being placed in prison or jail. Despite initial intentions, evidence exists that many alternative programs have little impact in reducing prison or jail incarceration because only extremely low-risk offenders are placed in these innovative programs. During the past decade, advocacy and development of alternatives to incarceration and community corrections grew by leaps and bounds throughout the entire country, and yet, the prison population also grew by 60 percent. Strong evidence indicates that an essentially two-track system of punishment is present in American society. Very low-risk offenders who would never have gone to jail or prison in the first place continue to be placed into these new, alternative programs. At the same time, incarceration continues to be used extensively for offenders that have historically been put into prisons. In addition, more recent evidence indicates that even less serious offenders are being now placed in prison more frequently in some jurisdictions.

Despite many who have promoted responsible alternatives to incarceration for over nearly two decades, this effort remains in an infant stage in regard to its actual impact upon reducing jail and prison overcrowding. It is extremely important that any effort to address the issue of prison and jail overcrowding must first decide how to establish a direct correlation between operation of locally based alternative programs and an actual reduction in incarceration. Specific communities will deal with this issue of retaining more offenders locally in a variety of ways. And yet, there do exist at least four generic strategies that any community must address.

The first key strategy is defining an appropriate group of offenders who are currently incarcerated but would be suitable for an alternative community sanction. Particularly because of the public's fear of crime and the perception that most prisoners are violent repetitive offenders, picking an acceptable group of offenders is extremely important in building public support behind such efforts. Several states have addressed this issue by identifying specific nonviolent offenses where a nonincarcerative sentence could be the preferred punishment and would not threaten public safety.

A second key strategy is establishing a clear rationale for retaining more offenders in the community through alternative programs. Is the rationale for the local community correctional program to rehabilitate the criminal or is such a program viewed as alternative punishment? The rationale determines to a large extent public perception and level of support the program can obtain. For example, if a local alternative program is designed to be a rehabilitation program primarily, it is quite likely that the public may view it as simply another criminal justice frill at best, and at worst, being soft on criminals. On the other hand, if the justifying rationale for the local alternative program is that of serving as an alternative penalty or punishment, public perception of the program and eventual support for that program are likely to be greater. To emphasize a community-based alternative program as fundamentally an alternative penalty or punishment is not to reduce the fact that it can also offer rehabilitative services to offenders. It is important, however, that the local program offers a practical, low-cost, and simple sense of justice in which the offender is held accountable for the criminal act and, whenever possible, the victim receives practical assistance and repayments.

Determining whether the local alternative program

should be residential or nonresidential is a third important strategy. Oftentimes, people equate alternatives to incarceration with such residential programs as halfway houses, work release centers, or drug treatment programs. Clearly, these programs are very much needed and should continue development in communities throughout the country. And yet, nonresidential programs in which the offender lives at home but during the day is involved in unpaid community service work, employment, counseling, and paying back his or her victim are equally needed. In fact, these nonresidential programs can have a far greater impact in addressing the problem of jail and prison overcrowding since they cost only a fraction of what it costs to place an offender in a halfway house program. The critical issue here is determining which offenders need the additional structure of a residential program versus those who can live at home independently while participating in a variety of highly structured responsibilities during the daytime. Obviously, public safety cannot be jeopardized in the process of responding to the dilemma of prison and jail overcrowding.

A fourth strategy in retaining more offenders locally is found in conducting a comprehensive public information campaign. Such a campaign needs to both promote the local alternative program and place crime and punishment in perspective. The highly emotional issue of crime should be desensitized through use of the mass media, speaking engagements before local organizations, and, particularly, radio and television interviews with victims and offenders that benefited from local alternative programs. The general public can then develop a more accurate and enlightened understanding of crime, a difficult and frightening issue.

The costly dilemma of massive prison and jail overcrowding in the United States remains the most critical issue facing the criminal justice system in the 1980s. There are no simple solutions, but as more communities work on developing local alternatives to incarceration, the issues identified above must be addressed. Particularly as the religious community begins to play a more active role in this movement, we should recognize that even though reconciliation between individual victims and offenders is a worthy end in and of itself, wherever possible, we must also advocate the broader issue of reducing the overreliance upon prisons in American society.

QUESTIONS FOR THOUGHT

1. Why are prisons and jails overcrowded?
2. Are prisons and jails primarily packed with violent, repetitive criminals?
3. What kind of problems result from overcrowding in jails and prisons?
4. Why do you think that federal courts have intervened in an effort to reduce the high levels of prison overcrowding?
5. If crime rates have stabilized and actually decreased in some jurisdictions, why are prisons and jails so overcrowded?
6. What role do sentencing practices by judges play in relationship to prison overcrowding?

7. Are there viable alternatives to sending certain offenders to prison?
8. If so, what type of offenders should be sent into the alternative programs?
9. What are the most realistic alternatives for offenders, rather than going to prison?

BUILDING JUSTICE AND RECONCILIATION

CHAPTER FIVE

BIBLICAL JUSTICE:

A Ministry of Reconciliation

*Hate what is evil, love what is right . . . and see
that justice prevails in the courts . . . Stop your
noisy songs; I do not want to listen to your
harps. Instead, let justice flow like a stream,
and righteousness like a river that never goes
dry.*

(Amos 5:15, 23-24 TEV)

It is not uncommon for people who remain quiet on
other social issues to express rather strong feelings about
crime and criminals. The simplistic "get tough" rhetoric,
which demands ever harsher penalties, and the growing
movement in support of capital punishment clearly
indicates this. Precisely because of the enormous fear
created by crime in our communities and the ineffec-
tiveness of so many of our policies of punishment, it is
important that the Christian community understand a
biblical perspective on this critical issue and respond out
of our Judeo-Christian heritage to the current reality of
crime.

71

A biblical perspective on criminal justice requires a review of both the Old and New Testaments. Many of those who believe in advocating harsher penalties, including frequent use of capital punishment, are quick to quote numerous verses in the Old Testament. Certainly there is a theme of vengeance throughout the Old Testament. We do not have to look very far to find that capital punishment was frequently used throughout the Old Testament days. In Exodus, God responds to Israel's disobedience with judgment and harsh punishment, including death for some. And yet, the theme of vengeance in the Old Testament is also tempered by the existence of other themes indicating the need to place limitations on vengeance and to exercise mercy and restraint.

Old Testament

The Old Testament reference to "an eye for an eye" is taken by many Christians to justify violent response to criminal behavior. And yet, a closer reading of this passage in the context of early Hebrew history indicates that the reference to "an eye for an eye and a tooth for a tooth" was to place proportionality into vengeance—clearly limiting the degree of retaliation for a criminal act. In other words, no more than an eye for an eye or a life for a life, was to be taken.

A detailed law related to crime and punishment was given to Moses on Mount Sinai by God (Leviticus 17–27 and Numbers 5–8). This law included frequent reference to what we now call restitution. The law given to Moses contained the foundation for compensation, liability, responsibility, and other ethical principles that are quite common to us in our modern world. In early Hebrew history, crime was viewed as a violation against a person, rather than the "state," and therefore, resolution must come between the two parties at conflict. Restitution was a procedure for righting the wrong. Reference is made to a thief's having to return the value of that stolen plus a 20 percent penalty (Numbers 5:5–8). In fact, the Hebrew word for restitution or repayment is *shalam*, which is the same root as *shalom*, the word that describes the state of a community characterized by justice, righteousness, and peace. Restitution in the Old Testament means to restore the state of *shalom*, to repair the breach in the community through again establishing wholeness, peace, and right relationships.

The frequent biblical theme of vengeance in the Old Testament is also tempered by a parallel theme emphasizing mercy for the offender. In order to avoid revenge by the victim's family, cities of refuge were to be established (Numbers 35; Deuteronomy 4, 19; Joshua 20). The cities of refuge allowed time for tempers to cool in order to work out a more positive resolution. The author of Deuteronomy states: "To me belongs vengeance and recompense," in reference to God (32:35, KJV). In Leviticus, once again the theme of mercy toward the offender is stated, "Do not take revenge on anyone or continue to hate him, but love your neighbor as you love yourself" (19:18, TEV). This theme occurs in other sections of the Old Testament and represents the initial foundation of the predominate theme of forgiveness and reconciliation in the New Testament.

As can be seen, the Old Testament is not simply a message of blood revenge and harsh punishment to those who violate the laws within our communities.

There clearly are counter themes emphasizing proportionality and restraint in punishment, restitution to the victim, and mercy to the offender. As Christians, we need to understand our Judeo-Christian heritage and how it is rooted in the Old Testament, yet, we need to also understand that we are Christian because of the fundamentally different message of the New Testament. The Old Testament message is rooted in a relationship between God and man characterized by law. The New Testament message communicates a very different theme in which the relationship between man and God is characterized by grace.

New Testament

Through the incarnation of God in Jesus Christ living in our midst, taking upon himself the sins of the world and ultimately being executed for his "criminal" behavior toward the religious and civil authorities, we no longer live under the burden of the law. Through grace and the unconditional forgiveness of our sins, we are now called to a new order where vengeance and retaliation have no place. In the Gospel according to Matthew, Jesus speaks of how "you have heard that it was said, 'An eye for an eye, and a tooth for a tooth.' But now I tell you: do not take revenge on someone who wrongs you. If someone slaps you on the right cheek, let him slap your left cheek too" (5:38–39, TEV). Jesus goes on to state that we are to love our enemies and pray for those who persecute us.

Jesus began his public ministry by quoting from the Book of the prophet Isaiah:

"The Spirit of the Lord is upon me.
    Because he has chosen me to bring good news to
    the poor.

He has sent me to proclaim liberty to the captives
   and recovery of sight to the blind,
to set free the oppressed,
   and announce that the time has come
   when the Lord will save his people
   (Luke 4:18–19, TEV).

The first act of Jesus' public ministry was a strong
declaration on behalf of social justice amidst God's
creation.

In the twelfth chapter of the Gospel of Mark, we read
that Jesus was asked which commandment was the
most important. Religious intellectuals used the
question to trick Jesus into a statement of blasphemy.
He responded with two simple and clear statements:
first, love God above all else with all your heart, mind,
soul, and strength; second, love your neighbor as
yourself (Mark 12:28–31). Jesus did not speak of
either/or. Rather, he emphasized a vertical relationship
with God through a life of faith, prayer, and worship,
and, a horizontal relationship between our brothers
and sisters of this world through a life committed to
social justice and human compassion.

A truly biblical perspective on criminal justice is
simply one expression of a broader and more holistic
understanding of Christian discipleship and the call to
servanthood. Such a perspective must not be simply a
one-dimensional definition of Christian responsibility
or a single-issue theology. Discipleship is anything but
simple and one-dimensional. As clearly stated by
Jesus, the presence of God in every aspect of our lives,
including the mental, the physical, the spiritual, and
the social is required.

As Christians, most of us are well aware of the need

for our vertical relationship with God. Our participation in prayer and worship is testimony to this realization. And yet, many of us have a far more difficult time understanding and experiencing the meaning of our horizontal relationship among our brothers and sisters of this world, as required by Jesus. In the letter of James, it is stated that if we see our brother or sister who is hungry and ill-clothed in need, we are not to simply offer some pious remarks about our faith, but rather to respond by offering food and clothing in order to meet immediate survival needs (James 2:14-17).

In a similar vein, Jesus speaks in the Gospel of Matthew about how we should not come to the altar to praise our God if we are not at peace with our brothers and sisters of this world. We are to first become reconciled with our brother or sister and then later come to the altar to praise God (Matt. 5:23–24). The apostle John says, "If someone says he loves God, but hates his brother, he is a liar" (I John 4:20, TEV). In short, our conversion to the lordship of Jesus Christ in our lives is multidimensional and requires both spiritual formation and social witness. Responding to crime and victimization within our communities simply must be one expression of our broader understanding of Christian discipleship.

There is, however, probably no other area of human behavior that is more difficult to understand or apply Christian discipleship to than that of crime. If we are honest with ourselves, many of us would have to admit that the crime in our communities and the persons who commit those crimes are repulsive. These people often represent the "scum" within our community, the evil people, the dirty people, the outcasts.

The Christian church is based on the fundamental concepts of love, forgiveness, and reconciliation. Most Christians are familiar with the parable of the good Samaritan in which we are given a clear definition of who our neighbor is, and required to show love to that neighbor (Luke 10:25–37). Our neighbor is not simply the easy to love, the familiar, the known, the person like us, but rather, the downtrodden, the rejected, the needy, the unknown and faceless people who are often "the least of those among us." Yet, despite our understanding of these basic concepts, how often do we really apply and experience these biblical principles beyond the comfortable boundaries of the church, or the people whom we find easy to love or forgive, whom we chose to respond to as our neighbor?

How do we love the person who has broken into our house and stolen our wedding gifts? How do we affirm as a child of God, worthy of forgiveness and reconciliation, the person who terrorized our family during a robbery? How are we to respond in love to the person who kidnapped, raped, and then killed our sister, when if we are honest with ourselves from the depths of our soul, we would probably cry out in anger for revenge, severe punishment—even, perhaps, death?

Perhaps nowhere in the New Testament is vengeance and retaliation so clearly repudiated as in the eighth chapter of the Gospel of John in which Jesus was asked to rule on the death penalty. A woman had been caught in the act of adultery by an angry and self-righteous crowd. Under Roman and Hebrew law, they had every right to stone this woman to death. This crowd of "good people" brought this "dirty and evil" woman to Christ for his judgment, prior to killing her.

Jesus looked that crowd in the face and stated, "let one without sin cast the first stone." In astonishment, the crowd dropped their stones and dispersed.

Jesus looked at the woman, forgave her, and told her to sin no more. Rather than affirming the death penalty, Jesus responded in a spirit of forgiveness and reconciliation. In doing so, he again violated the intent of some of the civil and religious laws of his day.

Perhaps Jesus gave his most demanding and threatening statement in regard to social justice and human rights in the well-known words of Matthew 25:31–46. Here he spoke of the final judgment and accounting before God, the fundamental concept of "inheriting the kingdom," of "heaven"—the cornerstone of the Christian church. On his right hand, Jesus addressed those who shall inherit the kingdom: "For when I was hungry, you offered me food. When I was thirsty, you gave me drink. When I was a stranger, you welcomed me. When I was naked, you clothed me. When I was sick or in prison, you came to visit me" (Matt. 25:35–36, author's translation).

Those on the left hand of Jesus were absolutely baffled. After all, many of them were followers of Jesus. In complete frustration, they cried: "When did we see you hungry or thirsty? You are our leader. You know we certainly would have given you food and drink. And when did we see you naked or in prison? Jesus, you know we would have helped you" (Matt. 25:37–39, author's translation).

Jesus responded sadly: "I tell you, whenever you did this for one of the least important of these brothers of mine, you did it for me" (Matt. 25:40, TEV). He made clear that an element of God, of himself, exists in each of us as part of God's universe and creation, regardless of our actions or inactions. We must hold sacred and seek to preserve all human life. Our insensitivity and coldness to the least of those among us—the outcasts and criminals—is also insensitivity and coldness to Jesus. The criteria for entering the kingdom of heaven is not religious ritual and piety; it is, instead, active discipleship and response to human suffering.

While the message offered by Jesus in the Gospel of Matthew 25 does not explicitly address victims of crime, nonetheless, it is relevant to victimization. Jesus can be found in those who are the least among us—the hungry, the naked, the sick, and the imprisoned. Do not victims of violent crime represent the least among us particularly as their security has been brutally and unjustly shattered by crime? Victimized and powerless before their aggressor, were they not in a sense naked? As these individuals recoil from the shock and trauma of personal violence, do they not hunger for our compassion, understanding, and support? Though it is difficult for us to respond to or even talk with victims of violent crime, are they not worthy of our visitation and support? Perhaps as Christ separates the sheep from the goats in the final judgment, our response to those who have been brutalized by crimes may also be a measure of our faith and discipleship.

Offender Accountability

Both the victim and offender are part of a social structure that, in a biblical sense, is in a "fallen state." As it was in the days of Jesus, governments preoccupied with power and military conquests today often display insensitivity to the poor and racial minorities.

The very social structure where victimization occurred may well have contributed to the criminal act by creating an environment of poverty, racism, and violence. Yet, as Dr.Robert Coates points out in an article in *Social Work and Christianity*, the fallen state of the world does not excuse the individual offender of his or her responsibility. Nor does it remove the community from the responsibility of holding its members accountable for criminal behavior. Dr. Coates says:

> As the Risen One, Christ represents hope for restoration and reconciliation. If we are to apply this reality of Christ-based hope to our victim-offender relationships, we have the cornerstone for restitution. The original goodness of the relationship has been broken; judgment and suffering are necessary, but there is also hope for restoration, i.e., reconstructing the relationship in a way that is enhancing to both parties.

The theme of reconciliation and forgiveness is found throughout the New Testament. Scripture does not communicate a naïve perception that there is no crime or conflict within a community structure, but rather, requires a fundamentally different response. Accountability for the violation that occurred can still, in most cases, be worked out through various forms of restitution.

In those relatively small but tragic percentage of violent offenses, such as rape and murder, restitution and accountability are certainly more difficult, although not impossible. Certainly, the deep emotional scar left in victims and survivors of violent crime can never be healed by restitution alone. Yet, perhaps financial restitution or reparation could be offered to the rape victim or the survivors of a murder victim to pay for various medical costs and related losses, while the offender is incarcerated. Even in those most heinous and tragic murders that we periodically read about, there is little in the New Testament message of Jesus to indicate the right of civil authorities to kill in return, as punishment. To the contrary, the ministry of Jesus in the context of responding to criminal behavior presents a consistent response of reconciliation rooted in forgiveness, rather than vengeance rooted in self-righteous anger.

Response to the Victim

Of equal importance is the New Testament implication of ministering to victims of crime. One of the most frequently repeated parables of Jesus relates to victims. We frequently think of the good Samaritan parable as primarily defining who our neighbor is, for this is the context in which Jesus offers this story. And yet, we cannot escape the fact that this parable speaks to the very essence of a Christian response to victimization.

How many of us would recognize ourselves in the priest and Levite who saw this man who had been beaten and robbed lying on the roadside and yet, continued on their journey past him? How many of us, like the Levite and priest, would rationalize such apathy and insensitivity because we did not know what to do or say to a person who had been beaten and robbed so tragically? How many of us would not take the time out of our busy schedules and important commitments to help this person lying by the roadside, failing to recognize him as a child of God worthy of our immediate attention and response?

It is interesting that it was the Samaritan, an individual who represented a despised minority population in that day, who exhibited such compassion. It is also interesting that the explanation of one of Jesus' greatest commandments, that of loving your neighbor as yourself, is rooted in the telling of this parable. The Samaritan represents a role model for modern day Christians in ministering to the needs of victims.

The Samaritan, by his example, tells us that as individuals we are to respond immediately in both offering compassionate understanding and practical assistance. This story suggests that providing a listening ear and empathetic heart to those who have been robbed or beaten or in other ways victimized is a very important ministry. This parable certainly indicates that more than a listening ear must be offered. Practical help for victims as they recover from the trauma of crime is extremely important—be it through financial assistance, transportation, medical assistance, or housing.

Justice Implications

Clearly, there are few other events in life that are more difficult to understand and respond to as Christians than the presence of crime in our communities. Many other important social issues must be dealt with by the church, and yet, as important as these issues are, oftentimes they do not pierce into the immediacy of our own lives and shake the very essence of our security and well-being. Unlike many other issues, crime can quickly enter any of our lives and with incredible swiftness create fear, anxiety, uncertainty, and insecurity. Bearing the pain and trauma can certainly be one of life's most difficult burdens.

A biblical perspective on the complex issue of crime and punishment recognizes the subordinate nature of the Old Testament theme of vengeance to the fundamentally different message of grace in the New Testament. For without the Incarnation of God, through Jesus the Christ, and his death and resurrection, the Christian church would not exist.

In attempting to distill the biblical implications for crime and punishment in modern society, I find several important themes. First, responding to crime in our communities must involve both the victim and offender. Since crime is fundamentally a violation between persons and relationships, the focus of the criminal justice system should not be solely upon the offender. While holding the offender accountable through various penalties is important, the legitimate needs of victims must also be recognized and responded to. And wherever possible, responding to the victim should not be in isolation from the offender.

Secondly, whenever possible the process should be personalized. Too frequently, both victims and offenders stereotype each other and respond in inappropriate fashions. Offenders typically rationalize their victims as "being rich," "their insurance will cover the loss," "after all, I didn't hurt anyone," and on and on. Victims understandably stereotype offenders as brutal, uncaring, and evil people who prey upon their communities and are of little worth. From a biblical perspective, we are all children of God, worthy of redemption. The *shalom* community cannot be restored

without personalizing the conflict between a victim
and offender and working toward a realistic sense of
reconciliation and repayment.

Third, in the pursuit of public safety and appropriate
penalties, the criminal justice system must not focus
exclusively on the crimes committed by the poor and
minorities. Any single criminal act is wrong, whether
the offender is rich or poor. Yet, continued massive
incarceration and, at times, execution of primarily
criminals who are "the least among us," while leniency
is frequently expressed toward the rich and well-
connected is a fundamental violation of the gospel
message of justice, reconciliation, and Christian
accountability before God.

Fourth, there should be reduced reliance upon
prison incarceration. Other than for physical restraint
of those extremely violent and repetitive offenders who
continue to prey upon innocent victims, there is little
biblical rationale for continued incarceration of so
many. This is particularly evident when policies of
incarceration are so closely linked to putting the poor
and minorities in our prisons, where they are
vulnerable to further violence, neglect, and despair.
Less destructive, nonincarcerative penalties must be
established. Alternatives such as intensive probation,
community service work, victim restitution, and work
release centers can hold many offenders accountable
while also strengthening the possibility of reconciliation between the offender and his community or
victim.

A fifth and final implication is related to the need for
Christians to be involved in an active ministry of
support and advocacy for victims of crime. For too
long, the major emphasis in much of the Christian

community has been solely upon the offender, particularly those in prison. Biblical justice is holistic. Jesus does not simply respond in compassion and forgiveness to the offender. He also provides a powerful message related to the pain and suffering of victims. Our nation's criminal justice system strongly reinforces the separation of concern for victims from concern for offenders. By definition, our adversarial system of justice divides people into "good guys" and "bad guys." Either you are a firm advocate of victims and therefore harsher penalties, or you are strongly concerned with the plight of prisoners and the need for rehabilitation. The Christian church must not fall into this trap.

Christian leadership must witness to the full meaning of reconciliation and redemption. Just as the church supports the need for creative alternatives to incarceration for many offenders, it must simultaneously be a strong advocate for victims and develop specific programs to address their many needs. Clearly, this is not an easy task given the extreme emotional sensitivity of crime and the oftentimes conflicting interests of victims and offenders. And yet, as Christians committed to a ministry of reconciliation, our collective efforts must be upon the reduction of rage and hostility among victims, as well as offenders. VORP, described more fully in chapter 7, represents one modest attempt at such rage reduction. Regardless of the difficulty of this task and the likelihood of being misunderstood by many within the criminal justice community and the broader public, our ministry must foster greater understanding between victims and offenders, while strengthening nonviolent conflict resolution techniques. Building upon the principles of both accountability and forgiveness, we must, in the words of the prophet Amos, let justice flow like a stream and righteousness like a river that never goes dry.

QUESTIONS FOR THOUGHT

1. Does the Old Testament reference to "an eye for an eye" provide Christians with a justification for harsh punishment of criminals, including capital punishment?
2. What was the meaning of the Old Testament reference to "an eye for an eye and a tooth for a tooth?"
3. What does Jesus have to say in regard to the notion of "an eye for an eye" in reference to punishing offenders?
4. What is the biblical meaning of reconciliation and peace as they apply to criminal offenders?
5. Is the biblical message related to criminal justice focused primarily upon offenders, or focused upon their victims?
6. What does the parable of the good Samaritan have to say in regard to criminal justice?
7. Does the response of Jesus to a criminal caught in the act of committing an offense punishable by death have any relevance to our modern day society? (See John 8:1–11.)
8. What are the principles upon which Christians should respond to crime and victimization within their communities?

CHAPTER SIX

A COMMUNITY RESPONDS:

The PACT Story

"I, the Lord, have called you and given you power
to see that justice is done on earth.
Through you, I will make covenant with all peoples;
through you I will bring light to the nations.
You will open the eyes of the blind
and set free those who sit in the dark prisons."

(Isa. 42:6–7, TEV)

Throughout this book we have seen the experiences and principles of PACT, (Prisoner and Community Together) at work. These remaining chapters take a more thorough look at both the organization and its various programs. Chapter 6 provides a brief overview of the history, philosophy, and overall development of the PACT organization. Chapter 7 provides detailed descriptions of three distinct program models developed by PACT over its fourteen-year history with an emphasis upon critical issues that need to be addressed by other individuals or organizations interested in replicating these programs within their local communities. This chapter highlights victim offender reconciliation, community service restitution, and residential (halfway house) program models. Finally, chapter 8 attempts to summarize the major themes of the book through proposing a more holistic strategy of justice advocacy.

While chapter 6 focuses upon the development of the PACT organization in Indiana, it should be noted that numerous other citizen-based organizations have been established to respond to the issue of crime and justice. The Parents of Murdered Children movement, the Offender Aid and Restoration organization with its numerous affiliates, the Southern Coalition on Jails and Prisons, the Minnesota Citizen's Council on Crime and Justice, and the Prison Fellowship movement led by Charles (Chuck) Colson are but a few examples.

The origin of PACT dates back to the summer of 1971 when a small group of citizens, including several ex-offenders, expressed concern about men being released from the Indiana State Prison in Michigan City, Indiana, with merely fifteen dollars and a prison-made suit. After a great deal of planning, a small federal grant was obtained through the Indiana Department of Corrections, and the PACT Community Resource Center opened on the west side of Michigan City in December of 1973. The center had an initial staff of five and provided residential, counseling, and employment services to approximately two hundred prisoners and ex-offenders per year.

In addition to the services provided at the center, PACT initiated educational and citizen involvement programs inside the state prison, as well as serving as an active public advocate on behalf of the rights and needs of prisoners and ex-offenders. Numerous justice conferences and workshops were organized; in addition the group responded to many requests to fill speaking engagements throughout the state.

As a community-based justice organization, PACT became actively concerned with building a more humane and creative sense of justice within its community. This was no easy task, requiring a holistic view of justice that recognized the full range of brokenness and alienation within the criminal justice system—affecting victims as well as offenders. PACT became concerned about promoting positive change in the individual offender, which could lead to lawful behavior in the community; positive change in community attitudes, leading to increased opportunities for ex-offenders and sensitivity to victims of crime; and positive change in public policy, leading to a more rational, humane, and effective criminal justice system. Strongly rooted in Judeo-Christian values and the active involvement of local Protestant, Catholic and Jewish citizens, PACT quickly embraced a philosophy of responding to the needs of individual offenders, while advocating a more equitable justice system.

PACT recognized that standing for justice is more than philosophy. It requires building tangible and real programs that represent effective models of community justice and reconciliation. The PACT organization began working for a number of ends: to make sure that men released from prison became successfully reintegrated into the community through employment, so that they would not return to criminal activity; to provide free community service restitution work as an alternative to jail for young offenders; to allow victims and offenders to become reconciled with each other and work out repayment agreements; to train community volunteers to visit prisoners and offer assistance; and to build public support for alternatives to jail and prison.

While PACT began as a small single program for men released from prison, because of requests for assistance from several other communities, it quickly grew to have a far broader impact upon the criminal justice system than its initial vision ever included. Several years after its initial origin, PACT began operating an ex-offender small business enterprise consisting of a day-labor contracting service. In response to a request from a local committee of church people, a judge, and a sheriff in Porter County, Indiana, PACT developed a local chapter to respond to the needs of prisoners in the local jail and to develop a community service restitution program. Chapter 7 describes this program in more detail.

A growing recognition of the important informational and emotional needs that victims faced within the justice system soon developed within the PACT organization. In conjunction with the local prosecutor's office, PACT pioneered the first victim/witness assistance program in LaPorte County, Indiana, through which many hundreds of victims received practical information about their cases and counseling assistance. Shortly thereafter, and in response to a request from local citizens, PACT established a new chapter in Elkhart, Indiana, which pioneered the Victim Offender Reconciliation Program (VORP) and continues to receive nationwide attention. This program has been referred to in previous chapters, and a thorough description of VORP is provided in chapter 7.

After more than a decade of involvement with thousands of victims and offenders the PACT organization is operating today a wide range of programs in twelve counties primarily in Indiana, but in northern Ohio, as well. With offices in several cities in Indiana (Michigan City, Valparaiso, Elkhart, Bloomington, and Paoli), and Lima, Ohio, the staff and volunteers of the PACT organization continue to struggle with bringing the powerful presence of reconciliation to the enormous amount of brokenness and hurt that characterize the criminal justice system—our nation's most violent and repressive social institution.

Both in PACT's early development and its current broadening impact in several states, the Christian community has played a vital role through individual members, local congregations, and larger, denominational support. The ministry of PACT has been able to reach an increasingly larger number of both offenders and victims, through a broad base of support consisting of Mennonites, Methodists, Quakers, Presbyterians, Lutherans, Disciples, Catholics, Baptists, and the United Church of Christ. The American Friends Service Committee, a national Quaker service organization was particularly instrumental in the initial development and support of PACT.

The current programs of the PACT organization include: Bradley House in Michigan City, Indiana, which provides residential and job services for men released from prison; Community Service Restitution Programs, which involve free community service work as an alternative to jail for offenders in the Indiana counties of Porter, Elkhart, Orange, Crawford, Harrison, Washington, and Floyd; Victim Offender Reconciliation Programs, which allow for face-to-face meetings of a victim and an offender, resulting in a restitution agreement, in the Indiana counties of Elkhart, Porter, Monroe, Orange, Crawford, Harrison, Washington, and Floyd, and Allen County in Ohio; and an Offender Services Program in Valparaiso, which provides assistance to prisoners and ex-offenders, including the preparation of alternative sentence plans. Several of the above mentioned programs are highlighted in chapter 7.

The broader concerns of the PACT organization both to provide assistance to local organizations developing their own programs and to serve as a nationwide advocate on behalf of criminal justice reform are addressed through the PACT Institute of Justice. As a separate unit within the PACT organization, the Institute of Justice trains many hundreds of individuals throughout the country in how to organize local alternative programs, provides on-site program development assistance in numerous communities throughout the country, works with local congregations and denominations in advocating and developing alternatives, produces and distributes written and audio-visual resources to a wide-range of individuals and organizations throughout the country and abroad, and operates a National Victim Offender Reconciliation Resource Center as a clearinghouse for training and information. In addition, the PACT Institute of Justice provides assistance to various state legislators through research and publication of reports on the issue of prison overcrowding and alternatives to incarceration, as well as, conducting research to assess the impact of community-based programs.

Building justice through nurturing a community-based organization from birth is no easy task. The vision, excitement, and idealism of the founders will, after time, be tempered by the harsh realities of organizational life and economic survival. Holding firm to advocating justice and reconciliation before the principalities and powers represented by the criminal justice system requires a strong faith in the power of our Lord to bring justice and mercy into the brokenness and carnage left in the wake of crime and punishment of criminals. It requires a persistent ability to work within an environment of what, hopefully, can be "creative tension"—a tension resulting from the difficulty in responding to the enormous human needs of both offenders and victims (including the feeling of being able to do so little) and the need to compromise. Often we must establish negotiated agreements to even have access to many offenders. It is a tension resulting from the frustration of trying to move beyond solely charitable action to specific individual victims and offenders and toward a broader advocacy of justice and reform of the criminal justice system—and the inevitable resistance to such advocacy.

While tension will certainly be present in the context of the external world of an organization like PACT in working on behalf of victims and offenders, such tension also surfaces within the organization as well. Moving from a young fledgling organization, fueled by a collective vision of justice, to a larger multi-jurisdictional organization with increasing complexity cannot help but trigger the whole range of human issues that any organization, including churches, faces. Ambition, greed, jealousy, insecurity, miscommunication, arrogance, insensitivity, and the inevitable grapevine of intra-organization gossip have all been part of PACT at one point or another.

Even in the midst of its efforts to advocate justice and strengthen the presence of Christian discipleship, many within PACT, including this author, have fallen prey to their own human weaknesses and insecurities. In short, building justice through an active commitment to Christian discipleship somehow did not reduce the vulnerability of Christian activists within PACT from being susceptible to the basic selfishness and sin that is part of each one of us. Dealing with this reality remains an ongoing concern and requires a good deal of flexibility in management.

Throughout the development of PACT, its organizational life has been characterized by open communication, intense work and play, and an abundance of creative energy. There were, however, at least two points in PACT's history where the very essence of the organization and its vision were threatened by painful internal conflict related to organizational leadership and direction. Had this conflict not been confronted and effectively brought to resolution through negotiation and leadership by its Board of Directors, PACT could have been destroyed. Each one of these incidents represented a death of part of the organization, followed by an enormous resurrection and rebirth of new energy, clarity, and a strengthened vision of PACT's commitment to justice and reconciliation.

From its inception in 1971, PACT has recognized that crime is often rooted in many of our community structures, institutions, and values, and its solution is ultimately to be found within our communities and their various resources. Simply warehousing certain offenders—primarily the poor and powerless—in prisons and jails is not viewed as the final solution by PACT, which recognizes the need to move toward increased use of effective community-based programs for the vast majority of nonviolent offenders. With no increased risk to the public, these community-based programs can hold offenders accountable for their actions, but also offer practical help in rebuilding their lives and repaying their victims. At a time when the nation's prison system is bulging and the cost of prison construction skyrocketing, PACT advocates greater use of alternatives to prison, which can offer more appropriate and less costly ways to punish many of the nonviolent criminals that continue to be packed into the overcrowded and ineffective prison system.

PACT recognizes that the demanding task of building a creative and realistic sense of justice, reconciliation, and compassion requires a broad and diverse base of public support, among the religious community particularly. Those who make up this broad base of public support include people who understand the need for a more humane and effective criminal justice system, one in which both offenders and victims can frequently benefit from through more positive forms of punishment, accountability, and restitution; people who recognize that while incarceration might be necessary for the most violent and repetitive offenders, it is not always appropriate; people who recognize that prisons are filled primarily with the poor and the minorities, literally those who represent "the least among us," despite the fact that crime abounds at all levels of society, with white-collar crime being far more costly than street crime; people who commit themselves to seeing that justice is done on earth, that light is brought upon the nation, and that release is brought to those who sit in dark prisons.

AUTHOR'S NOTE: Following preparation of this chapter, a number of significant and positive developments occurred in three PACT programs mentioned above. Elkhart County PACT in northern Indiana and Allen County PACT in northern Ohio (Lima) have become separately incorporated as local, private, nonprofit organizations, under the new names of Center for Community Justice and Victim Offender Services of Allen County, respectively. Monroe County PACT in southern Indiana is now under the leadership of the local probation department.

QUESTIONS FOR THOUGHT

1. What factors account for the beginning of PACT (Prisoner and Community Together) in the early 1970s? Are any of these factors present in your community?
2. What did PACT have to offer as opposed to what state agencies such as the courts and Department of Corrections were already providing?
3. Is there a role for private citizens within the criminal justice system?
4. Or, should the work of justice be left to professionals within the formal criminal justice system?
5. What do you see as unique in the PACT organization's approach to working within the criminal justice system?
6. How is PACT similar or different to other community-based justice organizations you may be familiar with in your community?

CHAPTER SEVEN

CRIME AND RECONCILIATION:

Three Models of Citizen Involvement

*"Happy are those who work for peace;
God will call them his children."*

(Matt. 5:9, TEV)

Throughout this book periodic reference has been made to either specific victims and offenders involved in the PACT (Prisoner and Community Together) organization or to programs operated by PACT in several Midwest communities. While PACT is a secular organization with a broad base of support, individual Christians have played key leadership roles throughout its fourteen-year history. This chapter focuses on three distinct program models developed by PACT through which offender accountability can be strengthened, and reconciliation with either the victim or victimized community can be worked at. In response to crime at a community level, a Christian ministry promoting reconciliation can take several different forms.

The most direct and intensive manner in which reconciliation can be worked at is through a face-to-face meeting between victim and offender. In this context, the criminal act becomes personalized as both victim and offender deal with each other as people, rather than stereotypes. The program model that PACT has developed and refined extensively over the years to facilitate these meetings is VORP (the Victim Offender Reconciliation Program). As such, VORP will be highlighted first and more extensively than the subsequent program models.

There are many cases in which a direct meeting between the victim and offender is simply not possible or desirable. In such cases, reconciliation can still be achieved through symbolic restitution in the form of unpaid community service work. Obviously, the intensity of both accountability and interpersonal reconciliation is far less in such a program. Nonetheless, PACT's Community Service Restitution Program model does provide a way to promote reconciliation between the offender and the community.

Finally, the third program model developed by PACT is Bradley House, a seventeen-bed residential program for men being either released from prison or sentenced to the program in lieu of incarceration. Providing a temporary home, counseling, and job assistance to ex-offenders is a critical need in many communities. Similar to community service restitution, this is a far less direct expression of reconciliation than a face-to-face meeting with the victim. However, increasing ex-offenders' capacities to become law-abiding citizens can oftentimes strengthen the likelihood of their reconciliation with and acceptance by the community they violated.

Victim Offender Reconciliation Program

The reconciliation that occurred between Fred Palmer and his victims, the Browns and Yohns (as described in chapter 1) is not simply a novel but isolated example of living out the Christian message of reconciliation and peace. Quite the contrary, more than a thousand victims have become involved in Victim Offender Reconciliation Programs (VORP) in different parts of the country. As with the Browns and Yohns, these victims, too, were able to meet the offender face-to-face, express their feelings of violation and frustration, receive answers to important questions lingering in their minds, and receive repayment through a restitution contract for the damages they incurred.

While the idea originated in Kitchener, Ontario, as a joint program of the Probation Department's Volunteer Program and the Mennonite Central Committee, VORP has been pioneered in the United States through the joint efforts of PACT and the Mennonite Central Committee, along with support from several other denominations, including The United Methodist Church and the Christian Church (Disciples of Christ), as well as a number of private foundations.

VORP was initially begun on a small basis by several Elkhart County probation officers and local volunteers. It was then developed more extensively through the Elkhart County PACT chapter, the Mennonite Central Committee, and the South Side Mennonite/Brethren Fellowship. VORP is an alternative process available to judges and probation officers for dealing with criminal offenders. It can offer a practical substitute for jail or prison incarceration. Meetings are arranged between victims and offenders, providing the opportunity for negotiation, reconciliation, and restitution.

Cases are usually referred to VORP by the Court and the Probation Department, although referrals may be accepted from other criminal justice, as well as community agencies. After a referral is received, reviewed by a staff person, and determined to be an appropriate case for VORP, it is assigned to a trained community volunteer. The volunteer separately contacts the victim and the offender, explains the program, discusses the offense and its aftermath, and solicits participation. If the victim and offender agree to meet, the volunteer sets and facilitates a meeting where the case is discussed, restitution negotiated, and a contract signed, stating the nature and amount of restitution agreed to. In addition, the victim and offender have a chance at the meeting to express their feelings about the offense, so that the conflict between them might be resolved. After the meeting, the contract and a written summary are sent to the referring agency for approval and enforcement. VORP keeps in contact with the victim until the contract is fulfilled.

VORP deals mainly, but not exclusively, with property offenses. Over 60 percent of the victims and offenders participating in the initial VORP in Elkhart, Indiana, were involved in felony offenses, committed by either juveniles or adults. The most common type of crime that VORP has dealt with over the years is burglary and theft. Cases involving such violent offenses as assault, armed robbery, and negligent homicide have entered the VORP program sponsored by the Genesee County Sheriff's Department in upstate New York and victims have reported their satisfaction.

7 1 2 2 6

This represents a particularly creative application of the VORP concept under the leadership of Sheriff Doug Call and program coordinator Dennis Wittman.

While the initial victim offender reconciliation program began in Elkhart, Indiana in the mid 1970s, with much nationwide and international media attention, as well as criminal justice interest in this unique program concept, VORPs since have developed throughout the United States and are now being tested in England and several other countries. With support from private foundations and several church denominations, a National Victim Offender Reconciliation Resource Center was established by PACT. This center provides intensive training to individuals and organizations developing VORP, and make a wide range of written and audio-visual resource material available.

Local VORPs are being developed in twenty states, representing more than forty local city or county jurisdictions, including Seattle, Washington; Fresno County, California; Wichita, Kansas; Minneapolis, Minnesota; Atlanta, Georgia; and Milwaukee, Wisconsin. In nearly all of these efforts, local congregations and individual Christians have played an active role. Serving as both staff and volunteer mediators, individual Christians have the opportunity of living out one of Christ's most fundamental teachings—reconciliation—within one of the most violent institutions in modern society.

As an alternative to costly and oftentimes dehabilitating incarceration, VORP provides a wide range of benefits to the victim, offender, and community.

The victim gets the rare opportunity to confront the person who violated him or her. This eyeball-to-eyeball meeting in the presence of a trained community facilitator, allows the victim to express feelings of frustration, hurt, and even anger. The victim may ask many practical questions. *Why me? How did you get into my house? Were you stalking me for a number of months? Why did you have to destroy my kid's toys? Was there something I could have done to prevent you from coming in?*

Beyond these emotional benefits, the victim is able to work out an acceptable form of restitution by the offender. In short, the traumatic experience of being a victim can be worked through and finally ended.

Offenders are held personally accountable by the VORP process. They are in the equally rare situation of having to learn the human dimension of their specific criminal acts. Even though they might just have stolen property, their acts still create fear and hurt within their victims. Meeting those they violated in a face-to-face confrontation is not an easy experience for many offenders.

VORP also allows offenders to avoid the destructiveness of what our nation's prison experience represents. Finally, offenders are given the opportunity to share their own humanity, to express sorrow, and to ask forgiveness.

The community at large benefits from VORP as well as the victim and the offender. With our nation's prisons dangerously overcrowded and building costs skyrocketing, finding realistic and appropriate alternatives to incarceration for appropriate offenders makes good sense. Taxpayers save money by supporting programs like VORP. Perhaps even more important, the presence of VORP in a community strengthens the teaching of nonviolent conflict resolution techniques. Nobody connected with the victim offender reconciliation process, be it the victim, offender, or mediator, can leave that experience without being moved by the creative power of reconciliation in human conflict.

Some might think that the victim-offender reconciliation process represents too radical a departure from the traditional criminal justice system in this country. Instead, VORP represents a return to fundamental Judeo-Christian values upon which our faith is built. Efforts to focus on personal accountability in response to community conflict and to emphasize restitution have a long history in Western civilization. Modern criminal law and its many legal abstractions, which define crime as being "against the state" and deemphasize the role of the victim, is a relatively recent development. As such, the victim offender reconciliation process can play a prophetic role in calling each of us to reaffirm some fundamental biblical truths of our Christian heritage and its application to modern life.

Key Points of VORP Model

1. Primary purpose is RECONCILIATION.
2. Secondary purpose is partial or total SUBSTITUTE FOR JAIL OR PRISON INCARCERATION.
3. VORP is not primarily a rehabilitation program for offenders. Rehabilitation is a byproduct of the reconciliation process.
4. VORP is deeply rooted in JUDEO-CHRISTIAN VALUES.
5. VORP operates best through a COMMUNITY-BASED ORGANIZATION (working closely with probation staff).
6. VORP involves a creative use of VOLUNTEERS as mediators.
7. VORP has a relatively low-cost budget.

Suggested Referral Criteria for VORP

1. Any felony case (adult or juvenile equivalent), primarily theft and burglary.
2. High-level misdemeanors, particularly if plea-bargained down from felony.
3. Identifiable victim.
4. Identifiable restitution.
5. Admission of guilt by offender.
6. Willingness of victim and offender to meet.

NOTE: the emphasis is placed upon receiving felony referrals into VORP in order to increase the ability of VORP to serve as either a partial or total alternative for incarceration.

VORP Program Statistics

NUMBER OF CASES	319
—Felony Offenses	63%
—Juvenile Cases	84%
—Adult Cases	16%
MOST COMMON OFFENSES	Burglary/Theft
NUMBER OF VOLUNTEERS	45
CASES RESULTING IN VICTIM-OFFENDER MEETINGS	60%
RESTITUTION AGREED UPON	$13,574
RESTITUTION PAID (closed cases)	$13,540

(Elkhart County PACT, Elkhart, Indiana, 1983)

VORP Case Example

Offense: Theft, $8,400 (Class D Felony, Indiana Code)
Offender: 21 year old (adult)
           Prior juvenile incarceration
           Several prior juvenile convictions (burglary, theft, status offense)

Sentence: (1) Community Service: 200 hours
(2) Victim Offender Reconciliation/Restitution
(3) Substance Abuse Counseling
(4) Jail Time: 161 days (time served awaiting trial)

VORP Case Example

Offender: Home Burglary (Class B Felony, Indiana Code)
Offender: 18 year old (adult)
Sentence: (1) Prison: 30 days
(2) Community Service: 180 hours of unpaid work
(3) Victim Offender Reconciliation/Restitution
(4) Probation: 7 years

NOTE: The other offender in this case received 10 years in prison from another judge.

Limitations of VORP Model

1. Because of the art of mediation required and its primary focus upon reconciliation, as well as the attention each case must receive, VORP is not a program that should be operated on a large scale directly by government agencies. With rare exceptions, experience has indicated that VORP works best when sponsored by a private organization working in conjunction with probation staff.

2. While VORP can serve as a partial or total substitute for incarceration for many offenders, it is not the solution to jail and prison overcrowding. At best, VORP can strengthen broader public policy efforts in limiting incarceration.

3. VORP is not an appropriate program for offenders who either refuse to admit their guilt or who display a strong, consistent attitude of arrogance and indifference toward their victims.

4. VORP is only for victims who are willing to participate. They must not be coerced.

5. While VORP works primarily with such common felony property offenses as burglary and theft, it also accepts a few referrals of more violent offenses in some locations (i.e., assault, armed robbery, criminally negligent homicide). However, the range of violent offenses to which referral to VORP might be appropriate is narrow.

NOTE: Extensive written and audio-visual resources and training materials about VORP are available from the:

> National VORP Resource Center
> PACT Institute of Justice
> 106 North Franklin Street
> Valparaiso, IN 46383

Community Service Restitution Program

In many cases, a face-to-face meeting between the victim and offender is simply not possible. Often, victims do not want to meet their offenders. Numerous crimes have neither a clear victim or a clear amount of loss that can be repaid. It is not uncommon for such offenders convicted of relatively minor property crimes to be locked up in a local jail, particularly if they have a prior record of arrests. Judges are frequently faced with no alternatives other than the extremes of probation as the most lenient sentence and jail or prison as the most punitive.

At the request of Judge Bryce Billings in Porter County, Indiana, and later, Judge William Bontrager in Elkhart County, Indiana, PACT developed its Community Service Restitution Program (CSRP) in the late 1970s as an intermediate penalty between the extremes of probation and jail. As an alternative to spending idle time locked up, an offender sentenced to so many hours of unpaid community service is involved in a symbolic restitution payment to the community whose laws he or she violated. Such a penalty is stiffer than traditional probation but far less destructive and costly than incarceration. Through a community service sentence, the offender can begin to work at righting the wrong committed, at becoming reconciled with the broader community.

The Community Service Restitution Program began in the cities of Valparaiso and Portage, Indiana, under the direction of Porter County PACT. It was later duplicated by Elkhart County PACT in the cities of Elkhart and Goshen, as well as by Hoosier Hills PACT in several cities of southern Indiana. For each day in jail, the offender received the opportunity to perform six hours of free community service work for governmental and private nonprofit organizations. A thirty-day sentence would result in one hundred eighty hours of free community work, which might involve painting a church, shoveling snow, working at a boy's club, or cleaning a county park. During 1983, a total of sixty local agencies benefited from over forty thousand hours of free work in Porter County, Indiana. This represented an economic benefit to the county of $300,000.

While community service sentencing has become one of the most popular criminal justice reforms over the past decade, with numerous state programs, few such efforts have been designed to serve as an alternative to inappropriate confinement. These programs often serve as an alternative to a fine or as an add-on penalty to probation. Both in its initial program design and through subsequent evaluations and changes, PACT, however, has attentpted to focus its Community Service Restitution Programs on jailbound offenders, particularly those charged with felony offenses. As a practical alternative penalty, there are several distinguishing characteristics of the PACT model.

Key Points of Community Service Model

1. Primary purpose is to serve as alternative penalty to jail or prison incarceration.
2. There is a clear separation of treatment (voluntary) and punishment (court ordered). Offender participation in treatment/counseling programs neither increases or decreases his or her responsibility to complete the total hours of community service ordered by the court.
3. Only convicted offenders who have already received a jail or prison sentence are referred to the program.
4. The portion of the jail or prison sentence that has not been suspended by the judge is then converted into community service hours at the rate of six hours for each day in jail.
5. The court sends a referral contract to PACT identifying the offender, initial jail or prison sentence and the community service hours required.
6. As a private, nonprofit agency, PACT is responsible for the program's entire administration.
7. Through active monitoring, major emphasis is placed

upon offender accountability in successfully performing the required community service.

8. Community Service Restitution Programs have a relatively low-cost budget.

General Referral Criteria for Community Service

1. Any felony case (adult or juvenile equivalent), primarily nonviolent offenses.
2. High-level misdemeanors, particularly if plea bargained down from felony.
3. Willingness of offenders to perform community service.
4. Maximum of three hundred hours of work ordered by judge, per case, with rare exceptions.

CSRP Program Statistics

TOTAL REFERRALS	150
—Felony Convictions	96
—Felony charge/reduced to misdemeanor	54
—Adults	115
—Juveniles	35
TOTAL COMMUNITY SERVICES HOURS ASSIGNED	19,272
AVERAGE HOURS PER CLIENT	100
PROGRAM TERMINATIONS	
—Successful	85%
—Special Circumstances	5%
—Unsuccessful	10%
ORGANIZATIONS RECEIVING COMMUNITY SERVICE	
—Private	23
—Public	13

(Elkhart County PACT, Elkhart, Indiana, 1983)

Community Service
Restitution Program Benefits

(Elkhart County PACT, Elkhart, Indiana, 1983)

- 14,069 hours of free work
- 36 community agencies receiving assistance
- 2,363 days diverted from jail/prison
- $101,480 economic benefit to Elkhart County
- Increased community involvement in criminal justice system
- Reduction of jail/prison overcrowding

Limitations of Community Service Model

1. Without a clear program design, targeting jail-bound offenders, community service can easily become an add-on to traditional sentences of probation for offenders who would never have gone to jail or prison in the first place.

2. Community service sentences have a greater potential than VORP to serve as a substitute for incarceration on a broader scale, administered by either private or public agencies. Yet, as with VORP, it is not the total solution to jail and prison overcrowding. At best, community service sentences targeting jail-bound offenders can strengthen broader public policy efforts to limit incarceration.

3. Without proper monitoring of offender completion of community service work, the program can easily lose its credibility as a viable alternative penalty.

4. Community service sentencing can become little more than a modern day form of the chain gang unless creativity is used in both developing various sites to perform work and encouraging on-site supervision of the offender by a representative from the organization receiving the work.

Bradley House

Getting released from prison and coming back into the free community is not a simple transition. With little money, few job skills, limited contacts, and often lingering bitterness about being locked up in prison, newly released offenders face a difficult situation. And yet, the successful reintegration of former offenders into the larger community was understood by PACT to be an important factor in promoting reconciliation between offenders and their community.

In Michigan City, Indiana, the site of the state's largest maximum security prison, Bradley House was established in 1973 as a fifteen-bed halfway house for men coming out of both the state and federal prison system. In addition to providing temporary residence during the difficult transition from prison to community life, Bradley House provides a supervised environment with practical counseling and job assistance. Formerly known as the PACT Community Resource Center, it was renamed Bradley House as a memorial to one of PACT's co-founders, Jim Bradley, who was an ex-offender himself. The program attempts to assist ex-offenders in achieving personal and economic stability within the larger community so that they do not return to crime. Only about 15 percent of the Bradley House residents have returned to prison because of further criminal activity.

Unlike many residential programs that operate on a "therapeutic community" model with intensive psychological counseling and therapy, Bradley House utilizes a practical, problem-solving model of service provision. A working definition of a problem is defined as a need plus an obstacle. Once obstacles are identified, specific problems are addressed. The problem-solving model used at Bradley House in working with ex-offenders consists of five basic steps:

1. Define the problem
2. Identify alternatives
3. Decide on *one* alternative
4. Act on the decision
5. Evaluate the decision

Individual client-service contracts are negotiated with the residents, focusing upon their self-perceived needs and goals. With rare exceptions, most contracts focus upon the need for employment, although a total of three goals per resident is required. In addition, job coaching workshops are offered to residents.

Community volunteers have played critical roles in the life of Bradley House. Often lay members from local congregations, these volunteers offer fellowship with residents through group gatherings, serve as volunteer instructors and tutors for residents, and assist in the actual management of the facility on weekends. The degree to which Bradley House can strengthen reconciliation between its residents and the broader community is certainly related to the active involvement of community volunteers including local congregations.

Key Points of Bradley House Model

1. Primary purpose is to facilitate successful reintegration of the offender into the community.
2. The problem-solving model of client intervention is used.
3. Client-service contracts negotiated between the resident and his counselor are the focal point of service provision.
4. Most referrals come from the Indiana Department of Correction for men who are within six months of the end

of their prison sentences or the Federal Bureau of Prisons. Some referrals come from the Federal Court as a direct alternative to being placed in prison.

5. Bradley House operates under the standards of the National Commission on Accreditation in Corrections.

Flow Chart of Resident Progress

ARRIVAL

INTAKE/ORIENTATION

CLIENT-SERVICE CONTRACT NEGOTIATED
(potential goals, three per client)
1. Employment
2. Education
3. Counseling
4. Fiscal Management
5. Housing
6. Community Referrals

WEEKLY COUNSELING SESSIONS
(contract monitoring)

CONTINUED PROGRESS TOWARD
GOAL ACHIEVEMENT

PROGRAM COMPLETION

Resident Profile (1981)

NUMBER OF RESIDENTS	64
—from federal prisons/courts	28
—from state prisons	36

AVERAGE LENGTH OF STAY	64.5 days
AGE RANGE	
18-25 years	38%
26-30 years	22%
31-35 years	23%
Over 35 years	17%
RACE	
—White	59%
—Black	38%
—Other	3%
EDUCATION LEVEL	
—Junior high	13%
—Some high school	26%
—Diploma/GED	45%
—Some college	16%
PRIOR FELONY CONVICTIONS	
None	56%
1-2	28%
3 or more	16%
REFERRAL OFFENSE	
—Nonviolent	77%
—Violent	23%

Limitations of Bradley House

1. Residential programs such as Bradley House are expensive to operate, because of the twenty-four hour provision of room and board, plus program services. While cheaper than prisons, few residential programs can operate for less than $100,000 per year, assuming a minimum of ten residents. Most will cost considerably more. As such, these programs are difficult to start by simply a handful of volunteers working.

2. Residential programs like Bradley House, or various restitution or work release centers, can clearly serve as alternatives to prison. And yet, because of their cost, far more offenders can be worked with through less costly

nonresidential programs such as VORP and community service.

3. Because of the enormous intensity in operating a residential program twenty-four hours a day, along with the emphasis upon resident responsibility, such programs can easily become preoccupied with "security" and "supervision" rather than quality service to residents.

4. With few exceptions, most residential programs do not yield as many practical benefits to either victims or the victimized community as nonresidential programs emphasizing restitution and community service.

Summary

Each of these three program models developed by PACT represent realistic ways in which citizens can become involved in the criminal justice system. They represent programs where Christians can be advocates of justice and reconciliation. None represent panaceas or simple solutions—nor are they exclusive to PACT. Religious and secular organizations throughout the country are developing similar programs. Each of these three program models do represent the fruits of one organization's labor through its fourteen-year struggle with responding to crime at a community level. Each model represents an effort by both Christians and non-Christians working together to reconcile the conflict between victims and offenders, at both direct and indirect levels.

QUESTIONS FOR THOUGHT

1. What does it mean to apply the principles of reconciliation to the criminal justice system?

2. What are the key characteristics of the victim offender reconciliation program developed by the PACT organization?
3. If you were a victim of home burglary, how would you feel about VORP?
4. Is VORP too soft on criminals?
5. How do you think offenders feel in facing their victim eye-to-eye?
6. What are the key characteristics of the Community Service Restitution Program developed by PACT?
7. How does the Community Service Restitution Program work at the principle of reconciliation and restitution?
8. How does a program like Bradley House contribute to reconciliation between the criminal offender and the larger community?
9. Do the program models developed by PACT have any relevance to your specific community?

CHAPTER EIGHT

JUSTICE ADVOCACY:

Key Organizing Issues and Strategies

"He has showed you, O man, what is good;
and what does the Lord require of you
but to do justice, and to love kindness,
and to walk humbly with your God?"

(Mic. 6:8, RSV)

In chapter 1, a very powerful and individualized story of justice and Christian reconciliation was described. In chapters 2 and 3 a broader perspective on the highly emotive and media-hyped issues of crime and punishment was given. The critical issues of prison overcrowding and the need for practical alternatives to incarceration were highlighted in chapter 4. In chapter 5, the biblical implications of working with victims and offenders were examined in the broader context of our Judeo-Christian heritage. The history and development of the PACT (Prisoner and Community Together) organization was offered in chapter 6 as one example of a citizen-based organization attempting to advocate justice and reconciliation in the communities it works in.

Three specific models of citizen involvement through alternative community-based programs which can strengthen the principles of justice and reconciliation were presented in chapter 7. These three models, developed by the PACT organization, and similar programs operated by other secular and religious organizations throughout the country, provide very tangible ways in which Christians can become involved in the criminal justice system. This final chapter will focus upon the broader principles and strategies of justice advocacy. Drawing upon the material in the previous chapters, the author's more than fourteen-year involvement with victims and offenders, and the writings of Dr. Robert Coates, chapter 8 will offer a holistic context in which Christians can become advocates for both victims and offenders.

As pointed out in chapter 5, Christian discipleship is not simply one-dimensional. Jesus does not call us to either love God with all our mind, soul, and strength, or to love our neighbor as ourself. In his summation of the greatest of all commandments, Jesus calls us to do both. Similarly, his ministry was not focused solely upon offenders or solely upon victims. The Sermon on the Mount, the parable of the good Samaritan, other parables of Jesus, and in fact, the whole Bible make it clear that a Christian ministry of reconciliation must bring healing and support to all those hurt within the criminal justice system, be they victims or offenders.

As we move from understanding crime and victimization and toward practical implications of Christian ministry, a number of critical issues must be addressed. Are we to minister only to the immediate spiritual and physical needs of victims and offenders on a one-to-one basis? Or, are we to be primarily advocates of reform in criminal justice system policies that affect victims and offenders on a broad public policy level? What does justice advocacy really mean and how can we be effective?

In the tenth chapter of the Gospel of Matthew, verse 16, Jesus commissions his disciples by telling them they must be as gentle as doves yet as wise as serpents. This verse has some powerful implications for Christian ministry and justice advocacy. Jesus' words imply that human compassion toward the poor and afflicted is a vital part of Christian discipleship. Yet, the implication that compassion must be tempered with wisdom and understanding suggests that compassion without wisdom in understanding the powers and principalities that control our lives can perhaps lead to simply "Band-Aid" solutions at best, or at worst, total irrelevance. In a similar vein, while wisdom in understanding the forces of evil is clearly also a vital part of Christian discipleship, without its being tempered by human compassion and care for individuals victimized by poverty, racism, crime, and numerous circumstances in life, such wisdom could be little more than cold and manipulative strategies at best. At worst, worldly wisdom, which is not tempered by a deeper compassion for the lives of individuals and a clear recognition of that of God in each one of us, can be little more than an expression of a cynical mind and a hardened heart.

Definition of Advocacy

Charity toward the poor and downtrodden has long been practiced by the Christian church, both collectively and individually. Reaching out to the afflicted is certainly important, as is having compassion toward those who are the least among us is unquestionably part of Christian discipleship. The practice of advocacy, however, goes far beyond the comfortable limits of charity. Just as charity is an expression of human compassion, advocacy is an expression of the wisdom necessary in dealing with the powers and principalities that affect the lives of those who are suffering in our midst. Whereas charity can oftentimes be practiced from a position of aloofness and paternalism, advocacy places us side-by-side with the person needing assistance so that we can together make a plea for fundamental justice—a justice that addresses the basic rights of all citizens in a free and democratic society; a justice that recognizes the need for equal opportunity and access to various resources in our society; and a justice that requires protection of certain basic individual rights by one's government. Whereas charity is often done "to" the poor or afflicted, advocacy is done "with" or "on behalf" of those who are suffering. Charity alone, as necessary as it is, can usually do little more than place small Band-Aids on immense social problems. Advocacy attempts to address the broader issues involved in why people suffer, while also trying to meet the immediate needs of those who are hurting.

The most generic definition of *advocacy* in human services is "acting on behalf of clients and/or client interest," according to Dr. Robert Coates in "Advocacy in Juvenile Justice: Concept and Practice." Several assumptions related to advocacy have been identified by Dr. Coates. These include the following:

1. Persons have certain inalienable rights: The right to essential goods to assure survival, and the right to develop their skills as long as they do not infringe upon the rights of others.

2. Each member of society should have equal opportunity and access to resources recognizing that individual variation will likely develop as persons use resources differentially.

3. Society has a responsibility to assure that these rights of persons are available to all of its members.

4. Advocacy needs to be defined broadly enough to encompass all the groups that carry out such activities.

5. Advocacy needs to allow for the development of self-advocates on equal footing with "professional advocates."

6. Direct service providers do and must continue to advocate on behalf of their clients.

7. The framework is built upon the targets of advocacy rather than the doers of advocacy.

Three specific types of advocacy are identified by Dr. Coates. *Individual case advocacy* focuses upon individual clients and the immediate needs they are facing. The role of an advocate in this context would be to work at linking the client with available resources in the community or attempting to change the manner in which such clients are dealt with by institutions or bureaucracies. Whether we are a community volunteer or a professional, individual case advocacy speaks directly to the immediate needs of individuals who are suffering in one form or another.

Community advocacy addresses the needs of a collection of individuals in a community with similar problems. Whereas individual case advocacy involves casework practice and securing of services on behalf of an individual in need, community advocacy involves basic community organizing and interest-group organizing techniques at a local community level. Community advocacy attempts to generate new resources for the clients it speaks on behalf of, and also tries to change various processes, such as local job training programs, educational opportunities, etc. that might discriminate. Community advocacy can also involve trying to link specific clients to various resources in the community, but at a less direct level than individual case advocacy.

Class advocacy is the third category identified by Dr. Coates. This form of advocacy addresses the concerns of a group of individuals across larger jurisdictional boundaries with similar problems. Rather than operating at a local community level, such as individual case and community advocacy, class advocacy usually works at the level of an entire city, state, nation, or even internationally. It involves coalition building and interest group organizing and focuses both upon changing processes that affect its clients as well as generating new resources. Because class advocacy addresses broad issues of public policy and needed reforms, it does not involve any direct linking of resources to specific individual client needs.

As can be seen, there are three basic goals that each of these three levels of advocacy address. These include:

1. Linking clients to existing resources—broadly defined to include education, skill training, jobs,

money, health-care, housing, and relationship support.
2. Generating resources where they are needed but lacking.
3. Changing processes that impinge upon access to resources, and on the manner in which clients are handled by public and private social service and social control agencies.

While there is an overlap between the goals of each type of advocacy, there is clearly a different emphasis within each type. Case advocacy obviously involves a much greater focus upon linking individual clients to resources, with a lesser priority on generating resources and broader public policy reform. Class advocacy, on the other hand, places a far greater emphasis upon broader public policy reform, with generating new resources for clients at a lesser level. Just as the goals of different forms of advocacy overlap, there are several other important commonalities. Dr. Coates identifies three such commonalities cutting across the three levels of case, community, and class advocacy.

The first is found in the very definition of *advocacy:* "acting on behalf of client interest." Clearly, it is important that each level of advocacy be closely related to client interest. On the one hand, this sounds rather simple. And yet, identifying client interest is not always that easy because of many conflicting self-interests that people who are suffering in one form or another may face. Advocacy in each of the three levels must continually work at clarifying specific client interest in speaking out on behalf of those needs, rather than getting caught in a more bureaucratic response that focuses upon simply processing cases and speeding up the efficiency of a system.

An important commonality is client participation in advocacy with professional advocates. It is important to have the client's input at each level, so that the practice of advocacy on behalf of their needs is rooted in concrete realities, rather than abstractions. Clearly, no one can speak more directly to "needs" than those whose needs they are. Direct participation by such individuals in the advocacy process can also be helpful in training them to be advocates for others in the future.

Relationship building is the third commonality that cuts across each type of advocacy. Good communication skills are needed in the building of relationships with the key individuals, organizations, and policy makers that can affect the circumstances facing a client. At a case advocacy level, addressing the immediate needs of individuals, the need for relationship-building with various social service agency representatives and other community representatives such as teachers and ministers seems rather obvious. Such relationship building is equally important in class advocacy. The ability to develop good and consistent relationships with key policy makers and politicians is a critical part in class advocacy leading to the successful reform of various public policies, which can have a dramatic impact on the lives of literally millions throughout our country.

Examples of Case Advocacy

A Victim Witness Assistance Program developed by PACT in a northern Indiana community in the mid

1970s represented a program through which individual case advocacy was practiced by both professional social workers and community volunteers. Frequently the forgotten ones within the criminal justice system, victims are often not even provided with clear information about the status of their case, about various continuances given the offender and court date changes—not to mention notification as to the final decision by the court. With rare exceptions, victims experience not only the immediate trauma of the offense, but also a good deal of anxiety as they go through the court system and its various bureaucratic requirements. The PACT Victim Witness Assistance Program and similar programs offer clear information about the status of their case to specific victims, attempt to link victims to various resources within the community, such as mental health counseling or financial assistance, and speak out on their behalf as they are processed through the court system. In addition, trained community volunteers assist numerous victims as they go through the court system. These volunteers both inform victims about what to expect and accompany the victims in the court room awaiting the processing of their case.

There are many examples of individual case advocacy related to offenders. One specific type is represented by the Alternative Sentencing Project operated by PACT. At the request of public defenders representing indigent clients who are facing prison, PACT prepares a thorough and well documented alternative sentence plan for presentation to the court, prior to actual sentencing. Such a plan will be tougher than normal probation, which is usually little more than a slap on the hand, yet far less destructive than long-term incarceration. Each alternative sentence plan is prepared in a client specific manner. Such options as community service restitution, financial restitution to the victim, counseling, employment, place of living, and other such areas will be addressed in the alternative sentence plan prepared for the court's review. While professional staff or consultants usually prepare such plans, including testifying in court during the sentencing hearing, community volunteers play a critical role as well. Many of these plans include a provision for a third-party supervisor who represents a community volunteer willing to work with the offender as he or she fulfills the obligations of the alternative sentence plan. Such a project is a clear example of individual case advocacy related to both linking the offender with existing programs and resources in the community and attempting to change the normal processing of such an offender—away from incarceration and toward a community-based program.

Dr. Coates identifies five different steps as critical in the process of successful individual case advocacy. First, it is important that you thoroughly know the case, the specific problem or issue facing the individual in need. Second, you must assess available community resources that may help this individual. Third, linking the individual's need and available community resources is critical. Fourth, it is important to teach those you are helping to be advocates for themselves in future situations. Fifth, you should follow up on the actual work prepared on behalf of the individual in order to assure effective implementation of your individual case advocacy strategies.

Examples of Community Advocacy

A growing community-based movement developed due to drunk driving and its impact upon both direct and indirect victims. The Mothers Against Drunk Driving organization (MADD) is a good example of community advocacy. Local chapters of MADD organize other individuals, particularly mothers, who have been victimized in one way or another by the reality of drunk driving and its resulting death and destruction. Basic community and interest-group organizing skills are used by many MADD chapters. Their efforts focus both upon generating new resources within the community to respond to the needs of victims of drunk driving, and trying to change the court processes related to drunk drivers. Frequently, MADD chapters monitor specific courtrooms and judges they consider too lenient and consider use of a variety of advocacy techniques to change the judges' behavior. This may include initiating a letter campaign requesting harsher sentences by the judge, a newspaper story about the judge's performance and the concern of the local MADD chapter, or even a major interview on a local TV station that attempts to show such leniency by judges. While MADD chapters may also be involved in individual case advocacy for specific victims, the major *emphasis* of such a group is usually upon changing court sentencing practices and getting more people to care about the issue of drunk driving in their communities.

In a small county in northern Illinois, a new organization called Youth Opportunities Unlimited was involved in a classic example of community advocacy related to service for offenders. This organization consisted of local citizens, including Christians, who were concerned about the need for a halfway house facility for juvenile offenders. No such services existed locally and the Youth Opportunities Unlimited organization believed it was foolish simply to send many of these kids away to state institutions.

With the development of any halfway house program, one of the most critical problems is finding a local facility the zoning board will accept. After surveying two cities within the county and numerous specific houses, in addition to talking with local key leaders and politicians, it became clear that neither of these cities would tolerate the placement of a halfway house for juvenile offenders within their community. With such clear opposition to the basic program being advocated by Youth Opportunities Unlimited, local organizers decided essentially to write off these two cities because of the extreme unlikelihood of ever getting proper zoning and to redirect their organizing toward a third city in the county.

Having learned a great deal from the opposition in the two previous cities, these organizers targeted key local politicians and influential people who would be willing to support their effort. The Youth Opportunities organizers also were able to gain full support of the city's mayor and a number of other influential leaders. Despite the presence of citizen opposition at the actual hearing, the zoning board approved unanimously the special zoning request for a group home to serve juvenile offenders. This program, which began in the early 1980s, has continued to grow. It has since moved to a different site within the city, and again, despite local opposition, the zoning board again has granted approval for a new site. The Youth Opportunities Unlimited organization represents a good example of volunteer citizens who advocate on behalf of the juvenile offenders within their community. Their efforts during this initial organizing process clearly were directed toward generating new resources within the community and changing the type of decision-making processes that often restrict the placement of halfway houses or group homes in local neighborhoods. Their commitment and persistence, despite negative experiences and considerable opposition, has paid off in the long run.

Community advocacy involves six distinct steps, according to Dr. Coates. First, a specific need must be identified and justified. Second, change targets must be identified, including both barriers and facilitators to the desired change. Third, the local political scene must be assessed, including an identifiation of key people who can significantly influence the desired change. Fourth, specific advocacy strategies must be developed. Fifth, the critical issue of timing is important—both for the specific interest group involved and the conditions of the external community environment (i.e., political campaigns, neighborhood conflict). Sixth, as with individual case advocacy, follow-up is very important to assure that the proper strategies are used.

Examples of Class Advocacy

Whereas case and community advocacy focuses upon either the individual or the local community, class advocacy represents a far broader attempt to bring about change. MADD not only represents a good example of community advocacy, but also offers a clear example of class advocacy from a victim perspective.

MADD has developed an extensive nationwide network of local chapters, all of which play active roles in changing state and federal laws related to drunk driving. In fact, much of the changing court practices toward drunk drivers, through legislative enactment of harsher penalties, can be attributed to the effectiveness of MADD serving as a reform advocate on behalf of the entire class of those who have been victimized or may be vicitmized in the future by drunk driving. In recent times, few other issues and related organizations have been so effective in extending a grass-roots organization into a nationwide network that has effectively changed sentencing practices. This is an excellent example of class advocacy, since MADD clearly represents individuals across much larger jurisdictional boundaries and effectively changes court sentencing practices.

Another example of class advocacy from a victim's perspective can be found in the example of the Parents of Murdered Children organization. While PMC has not been as active in the legislative arena as MADD, it has played a vocal and active national role in advocating through the media, as well as before state and federal governments, that more sensitivity and concern be shown toward the survivors of murdered children. A recent example of this class advocacy is represented by the testimony of Charlotte Hullinger, co-founder of PMC, before the President's Commission on Victimization.

The passage of the Indiana Community Corrections Act by the Indiana General Assembly in 1979 is directly related to a strategy of class advocacy developed by PACT. Representing the entire class of particularly nonviolent offenders in Indiana, PACT, through its

Community Corrections Advocacy Project, played an active role in researching, advocating, and implementing this new piece of legislation. The legislation provides state funds as an incentive to local communities who are willing to punish nonviolent offenders within the community rather than sending them to overcrowded state facilities.

The early development of this strategy of class advocacy was rooted in research done by PACT in several other states. It involved the review of model legislation, the preparation and distribution of several major reports advocating the passage of such a law and indicating its projected impact upon the Indiana criminal justice and corrections system, as well as actual testimony before various state legislative bodies. The entire process of this class advocacy spanned nearly five years, and culminated in the appointment by the governor of a special legislative committee to examine alternatives. This special legislative committee, frequently drew upon the research and experience of PACT during its analysis stage and in its final drafting of recommendations. Without this special legislative committee it is unlikely the law would have been implemented to the full extent that it eventually was. In addition, PACT played an active role in the actual drafting of the legislation through the appointment of its executive director to the Governor's Corrections Code Commission.

As with case and community advocacy, there are a number of critical, and in some respects, similar steps in class advocacy. First, there is a need to define and document the issue to be addressed. Second, the specific change targets must be identified, including barriers to desired reform as well as factors that might facilitate that reform. Third, the political environment must be assessed and clearly understood. Four, specific advocacy strategies must be selected. Ask such questions as whether or not direct legislative efforts should be made, is your organization able to lobby, how much grass roots organizing should occur, and should there be active media (newspaper, radio, and television) critiques of the issue and figures involved in the issue. Fifth, an analysis of key leaders must occur in order to assess their potential support as well as the ability to neutralize active opposition. Sixth, as with other types of advocacy, timing is absolutely critical. And finally, follow-up must occur.

Summary

The critical factor in understanding advocacy as part of Christian ministry in the criminal justice system is to view its practice not as an *either/or* proposition. Too often we are either concerned about the individual needs of a specific client (be they victim or offender), or we are concerned only about broad social change and therefore must focus on class advocacy. However, Christian discipleship and ministry is multidimensional. Working with victims and offenders must be part of a holistic concern for justice and the presence of God's kingdom in our midst. While the above examples provide brief glimpses into the various levels of advocacy, there are countless other examples relating to Christian ministry among victims and offenders. Participation of Christians as advocates for justice and reconciliation through any of these ministries with victims and offenders represents an important manifestation of Christian discipleship.

The extent to which we advocate and perform our ministry in a solely one-dimensional and individualistic context, oblivious to the hurt and injustice that similarly affects so many others in the same field, certainly limits the contribution of such efforts to a more healthy and healing ministry of Christian intervention. On the other hand, to the extent that we take seriously our Lord's directive to be both as gentle and harmless as doves and as wise as serpents in understanding the forces around us through a multi-dimensional ministry of advocacy with both individuals, the community-at-large, and broader policies adopted by our government, we greatly strengthen the powerful presence of Christ in offering reconciliation and peace to a broken and suffering world.

QUESTIONS FOR THOUGHT

1. How is justice advocacy different from charity?
2. What does *advocacy* mean?
3. Are there different types and levels of justice advocacy?
4. How can one organization be an advocate for both victims and offenders?
5. Have you ever been involved in an organization where you played an advocacy role on behalf of juvenile or adult offenders?
6. Have you ever fulfilled the role of an advocate for a victim of a crime?
7. Should Christians offer relief to individual victims and offenders through acts of charity, or should they serve as advocates of a broader sense of social justice within society?

8. Is it possible or appropriate for Christians to do both?
9. What are key organizing issues to address while advocating within the justice system?
10. How can your church or community organization serve as an advocate for victims and/or offenders within your community and state?

RESOURCES

I. Organizations

PACT Institute of Justice
National Victim-Offender
Reconciliation Resource Center
106 North Franklin
Valparaiso, IN 46383
(219) 464-1400

Office of Criminal Justice
Mennonite Central Committee
220 West High Street
Elkhart, IN 46516
(219)293-3090

Prison Fellowship
Box 40562
Washington, DC 20016
(703) 759-4521

National Interreligious Task Force on Criminal
Justice (National Council of Churches)
476 Riverside Drive, Room 1700A
New York, NY 10015

National Council on Crime and Delinquency
760 Market Street, Suite 433
San Francisco, CA 94102
(415) 956-5651

Parents of Murdered Children
1739 Bella Vista
Cincinnati, OH 45237
(513) 242-8025
Offender Aid & Restoration/USA
409 East High Street
Charlottesville, VA 22901
(804) 295-6196
Southern Coalition on Jails and Prisons
P. O. Box 120044
Nashville, TN 37212
(615) 383-9610

II. Booklets and Journal Articles

Challenges to the Injustice of the Criminal Justice System: A Christian Call to Responsibility. A policy statement of the National Council of Churches, November 10, 1979. (Available from JSAC, 475 Riverside Drive, Room 1700A, New York, NY 10115.)

Coates, Robert B. *Advocacy in Juvenile Justice: Concept and Practice.* 1983. (Available from PACT National VORP Center.)

————. "Victim-Offender Restitution as Viewed through the Theology and Ethics of Dietrich Bonhoeffer." *Social Work and Christianity*, 9, December 1982.

Colson, Charles W. *Is There a Better Way: A Christian Perspective on Prisons and Alternatives.* Prison Fellowship, P. O. Box 40562, Washington, DC 20016.

Colson, Charles W. and Daniel H. Benson. "Restitution as an Alternative to Imprisonment." *Detroit College of Law Review*, 2, 1980.

Jackson, Dave. "Victims of Crime Turn the Other Cheek." *Christianity Today*, April 9, 1982. (Available from PACT National VORP Center.)

Overcrowded Time: Why Prisons Are So Crowded and What Can Be Done. Edna McConnell Clark Foundation, 250 Park

Avenue, New York, NY 10017, 1982. (Also available from PACT National VORP Center.)

Umbreit, Mark. "Reconciling Victims and Offenders: A Practical Christian Justice Ministry." *Engage/Social Action*, a journal of The United Methodist Church, February 1982.

———. "Victim-Offender Reconciliation Is Ultimately Practical." *Christianity Today*, April 9, 1982. (Available from National VORP Center.)

The VORP Book, a comprehensive technical assistance manual for those interested in developing a Victim-Offender Reconciliation Program, 1983. (Available from PACT National VORP Resource Center.)

Zehr, Howard. *The Christian as Victim*. Mennonite Central Committee. (Available from PACT National VORP Center or MCC.)

———. *Mediating the Victim-Offender Conflict*. Mennonite Central Committee. (Available from PACT National VORP Center or MCC.)

Zehr, Howard, and Mark Umbreit. "Victim-Offender Reconciliation: An Incarceration Substitute?" *Federal Probation Journal*, December 1982. *(Available from PACT National VORP Center.)*

NOTE: Unless otherwise noted, copies of the above articles are available from the PACT National Victim-Offender Reconciliation Resource Center.

III. Books

Alper, Benedict S., and Lawrence T. Nichols. *Beyond the Court Room: Programs in Community Justice and Conflict Resolution*. Lexington, Mass.: Lexington Books, 1981.

Bard, Morton, and Dawn Sangry. *The Crime Victim's Book*. New York: Basic Books, 1979.

Colson, Charles W. *Life Sentence*. Waco: Tex.: Chosen Books, 1979.

DeWolf, L. Harold. *What Americans Should Do about Crime*. New York: Harper & Row, 1976.

Instead of Prisons. Mack Morris, ed. Syracuse, N.Y.: Prison Research Education Action Project, 1976.

Jackson, Dave. *Dial 911: Peaceful Christians and Urban Violence.* Scottsdale, Pa.: Herald Press, 1981.

Mackey, Virginia. *Punishment: In the Scripture and Tradition of Judaism, Christianity and Islam.* Rochester, N.Y.: National Inter-Religious Task Force on Criminal Justice, 1981.

Magee, Doug. *What Murder Leaves Behind: The Victim's Family.* New York: Dodd, Mead & Co., 1983.

McHugh, Gerald Austin. *Christian Faith and Criminal Justice.* New York: Paulist Press, 1978.

Reiman, Jeffrey H. *The Rich Get Richer and the Poor Get Prison.* New York: John Wiley & Sons, 1979.

Silberman, Charles E. *Criminal Violence, Criminal Justice.* New York: Random House, 1978.

Wilkinson, Henrietta, and William Arnold. *Victims of Crime: A Christian Perspective.* Published by the Presbyterian Criminal Justice Program of the Presbyterian Church, U.S. and United Presbyterian Church, U.S.A., 475 Riverside Drive, New York, N.Y. 10115, 1982.

IV. Slides (including narrative cassette and script)

Crime: The Broken Community was developed by the Mennonite Central Committee's Office of Criminal Justice. This slide presentation looks briefly at the criminal justice process from the point of view of the victim, the offender, the judge, and the Bible—stressing the need for new alternatives that allow for restitution and repair. Designed as an introductory film for discussions of alternatives, the church's involvement in criminal justice, and the Victim-Offender Reconciliation Program. (Approximately 12 minutes.)

Crime: Mediating the Conflict is a slide presentation focusing specifically on the Victim-Offender Reconciliation Program, demonstrating the process by following the story of an actual case. This slide presentation, also developed by MCC, may be used in conjunction with *Crime: The Broken Community* or as an individual presentation. (Approximately 12 minutes.)

Criminal Punishment: Prisons or Alternatives? was produced by PACT to highlight the problem of prison overcrowding and the potential of alternatives to incarceration. This presentation features such programs as Community Service Restitution Programs, Victim-Offender Reconciliation Programs, and residential programs. Excellent for presentation to business groups, civic clubs, and criminal justice officials. (Approximately 14 minutes.)

Slides may be rented or purchased at the following rates:
Rental—$10   Purchase—$35
(Available from PACT National VORP Center.)

V. Video Tapes (1/2 inch VHS and 3/4 inch tapes available)

NBC Today Show/Hour Magazine Show tape features the VORP program through interviews with actual victims, offenders, and Mark Umbreit, President of PACT. Interviews are with Phil Donahue on the *Today Show* and with Gary Collins for *Hour Magazine*. (Approximately 25 minutes.)

Newsmakers Show tape, produced by the ABC affiliate in Indianapolis, features clips from the VORP training tape, an interview with Mark Umbreit, President of PACT, and Evelyn Ridley, Supervisor of Community Corrections Services for the Indiana Department of Corrections. Topics include VORP and other alternatives as opposed to a traditional sentence, impact on program participants as well as on the overall criminal justice system, and views of the Department of Corrections on such programs. This is a particularly good tape to relate the VORP concept to the broader issue of jail and prison overcrowding. (Approximately 30 minutes.)

"Going Straight," a nationwide documentary produced by ABC and Dave Bell Associates and narrated by George

Kennedy, deals with the issue of alternatives to incarceration by highlighting three programs currently in operation in the U.S. Included in these three programs are the National Center on Institutions and Alternatives, Earn-It Program in Massachusetts, and VORP in Elkhart, Indiana: This tape is a good educational tool that addresses the practical benefits of alternative punishments. (Two versions: 30 minutes and 50 minutes.)

"VORP Mediation Training" tape, jointly produced by PACT and the Kitchener, Ontario, VORP, offers several simulations on the various facets of mediating a meeting between the victim and offender. These simulations provide examples of gaining victim participation, exploring facts and feelings of both the victim and offender, regulating the interaction between the victim and offender, introducing restitution, and reaching agreement. An excellent training piece, this tape can also be used as a basic education tool for individuals with some knowledge of VORP. (Approximately 35 minutes. A written guide for using the training tape is also available.)

CBS (Washington, D.C.), "People Are Talking" (Maryland.) The CBS production is a five-part series on prison overcrowding in the DC/Maryland area aired as part of the CBS evening news. PACT's VORP is highlighted in one episode as being one of the positive alternatives to incarceration. The "People Are Talking" talk show, originating in Baltimore, features an interview with an actual victim and offender, as well as with PACT's Executive Director. (Approximately 20 minutes.)

"The Sentence of the Court," a BBC (London) Documentary/Canadian VORP Training Tape. This documentary deals with prison overcrowding in England and the dilemma over the incarceration of nonviolent offenders—a major contributor to the overcrowded British system. VORP in Elkhart, Indiana, is highlighted in this documentary as one alternative to incarceration for nonviolent offenders. The Canadian training piece features a mediation meeting between victim and offender facilitated by a volunteer. (Approximately 75 minutes—BBC: 60 minutes, Canadian Training: 15 minutes.)

CBS (Buffalo, N.Y.) "Crisis Behind Bars" is a series of reports on prison overcrowding that appeared on the CBS evening news. The series looks at the problem of prison overcrowding, as well as several ways to alleviate this overcrowding. The Victim-Offender Reconciliation Program is highlighted, along with the Community Service Restitution Program of the Genesee County Sheriff's Department in upstate New York. (Approximately 20 minutes.) Video tapes may be rented at $35 per tape. (Available from PACT National VORP Center.)